There can be no doubt tha  ive
sustained withering attacks My
friend, Pastor David Lazo, i iile
the devil destroys marriage of
Love as a righteous prescription for every married couple that has
been weakened by a rushing tide of immorality and hopelessness.
He leaves no detail unattended as he provides an effective antidote
to the diabolical onslaught against the God-ordained institution of
marriage.

Husbands and wives, whether they are newly married or have been
together for decades, will benefit from his wisdom and insight about
how to develop and maintain a strong and vibrant marriage.

DR. ROD PARSLEY
FOUNDER & LEAD PASTOR
WORLD HARVEST CHURCH - COLUMBUS, OH

Never before in the history of the world has the institution of marriage
come under attack as it is today. The statistics are discouraging and
the attacks are relentless causing so many to have absolutely no
hope. In Steps of Love, Pastor David Lazo has written a practical
guide to change that. Every couple that reads and applies the steps
in this book will benefit from the solid Biblical foundation that
he speaks from. Regardless of what state you find your marriage
currently in, you will find a remedy for the challenges you face as a
couple. I encourage you to read Steps of Love with confidence and
with hope and watch what God can do.

PASTOR MARK COWART
CHURCH FOR ALL NATIONS/COLORADO SPRINGS, CO

Dr. Lazo did it again! If you need to turn up the heat in your
marriage or fire up your relationship with the Lord Jesus, this book
will get it done. In these pages you will benefit from his coaching

and be encouraged by his step-by-step action plan." Please buy two books...one is yours to keep, the other becomes a gift for the couple you care about the most!"

PASTOR MIKE SILVA | PRESIDENT OF MIKE SILVA INTERNACIONAL

Have you been looking for a simple manual on how to survive and succeed in your marriage? Then, this is the book for You! David and Raquel have been used by God to save countless marriages and make others solid and lasting. It has been my honor to know them for several decades. In David's book "The Steps of Love," he explains how a husband and wife can love each other in such a practical and straightforward format. This truly is a "how to do" book that teaches you to be a better husband or wife. After you and your spouse read this book, you will have plenty of opportunities to put it into use. I highly recommend the "Steps of Love" for every married couple; it is literally the best manual on marriage I have ever read.

TOM BARKEY, PH.D.
LEAD PASTOR
CHURCH OF GRACE

In his book, "Steps of Love" Dr. Lazo literally takes us by the hand and shows us the path to a more successful and fulfilled marriage. Very few people I know can explain the construct of love and marriage like Dr. Lazo. If you are serious about taking the necessary steps in order to have a long and life-giving relationship with your spouse, this is a must read.

JAIME LOYA LEAD PASTOR
CROSS CHURCH SAN BENITO, TEXAS

THE STEPS OF
LOVE

HOW TO IGNITE THE PASSION FOR INTIMACY

DAVID LAZO

Unidos en Amor

The Steps of Love
How to Ignite the Passion for Intimacy
© 2022 by David Lazo

Printed in the United States of America.
ISBN-13: 979-8-9855727-0-4
LCCN: 2022900671

 Unidos en Amor

Introduction

Being in love means desiring the absolute happiness of your spouse, admiring them for the individual they are, and feeling motivated to be a better person for them. When you are in love, your relationship goes beyond a simple physical attraction. To have a long-lasting and fulfilling marriage, requires learning to take the proper steps of love that stem from the Word of God. If you, as a married couple, can practice these fifteen steps of love that the Bible teaches, you will be able to have a healthy and wonderful marriage.

"Love is patient and kind. Love is not jealous or boastful or proud or rude. It does not demand its own way. It is not irritable, and it keeps no record of being wronged. It does not rejoice about injustice but rejoices whenever the truth wins out. Love never gives up, never loses faith, is always hopeful, and endures through every circumstance. Prophecy and speaking in unknown languages and special knowledge will become useless. But love will last forever....

three things will last forever—faith, hope, and love—and the greatest of these is love."

(1 CORINTHIANS 13: 4-8, 13)

God established these principles to help us stand firm in the structure of love. Therefore, love itself, becomes the foundation of a union between a husband and wife. We know that it's not possible to build a secure building without a solid, firm foundation. In this book, I will teach you how to build a strong healthy foundation regarding love.

To have a healthy and effective marriage, love must be nurtured, cared for, and above all else, it must be strengthened. As a pastor and marriage counselor, I notice the lack of a genuine love in the union of couples today. Love is the main factor that has been eliminated between a husband and wife. Love has become more of a myth, a fantasy, a means for sexuality or intimacy, rather than honoring and respecting the marital union. This is the cause for so many divorces in our society. All due to the simple reason that love is currently at a point of extinction since many couples have lost the romance, eliminated the values, and the respect in the marriage.

I hope that this book helps you revive the genuine love that God established since the beginning, when he constituted marriage. The key is in Jesus's greatest example. He loved the church in such a way that he gave himself for it:

"Husbands, love your wives, just as Christ also loved the church and gave Himself for her." (Ephesians 5:25, NIV)

Love is a total surrender, a sacrifice till death. It is my hope that *The Steps of Love* will help to reaffirm, revive, and strengthen the love in your marriage.

TABLE OF CONTENTS

CHAPTER 1

PREPARING THE ATMOSPHERE

> **"Cherish her, and she will exalt you; embrace her, and she will honor you."**
>
> **PROVERBS 4:8 (NIV)**

I can vividly recall the day that I met my beautiful wife, Raquel. It was totally unexpected but most assuredly, a gift from heaven. During our courtship I learned how to be a gentleman, how to respect her and how to please her desires. It was a very romantic courtship. She lived in San Diego, California, and I lived in Anaheim, California, the distance that separated us was of two hours. This was difficult for me as a young man who didn't have transportation, but that did not stop me from going to see her.

We communicated through letters and phone calls. Without fail, each week I would receive a letter from her, scented with her favorite perfume, and every night as I went to bed, I could sense her presence near me. Whenever we spoke on the phone, her voice and her words would excite me, and I became more attracted to her. For our three-month anniversary, which was a very special moment for us, I sent her a dozen red roses. During the process of our relationship, I learned to conquer Raquel by pleasing her likes and prepare our time together near the beach, her favorite place.

Though many decades have passed, the flame continues to burn within us. I have learned to be sensible to her needs, tastes, desires, her moments, and most of all, the importance of the quality time we spend together. She is the woman I chose to live with for the rest of my life. She is my best friend, my lover, my companion, my longing, my treasure, the mother of my children; but more than anything else, she has been and continues to be my one true love.

Now that our children are grown adults with their own families, Raquel and I have embarked on an extended second honeymoon during this stage of our lives. We are no longer the same physically, our emotional needs have changed, yet the atmosphere is still very much the same. I am referencing the romance atmosphere. The dictionary describes the word atmosphere as the layer of air that covers the earth. When I use the word atmosphere regarding romance, I am referencing the layer of love that covers the place where two people in love are present.

The Issue with Men

We as men, do not necessarily understand the need for a romantic atmosphere. After all, why do we need to be romantic with our wives when we have already won their hearts? That is the issue most men have today. The concept of romance has disappeared from the vocabulary of many men. So without a continual felt need for a romantic atmosphere, there will be little or no romance.

Wives, on the other hand, tend to seek and appreciate romantic settings with their husbands; a passionate atmosphere full of sweet words to make them smile, soothing music to soften the mood, candles to illumine the soul, and last but not least, spontaneous kisses that reveal a deep, abiding love for each other. I am not referring here to the act of sexual intimacy itself, but rather to the need for preparing a romantic atmosphere prior to that ultimate physical oneness.

When reading Esther 2:12, we learn how women were prepared to present themselves to the king. This illustrates the importance of preparing the atmosphere: *"Before each young woman was taken to the king's bed, she was given the prescribed twelve months of beauty treatments — six months with oil of myrrh, followed by six months with special perfumes and ointments."*

Atmosphere has much to do with the preparation of the presentation. This includes how a woman looks, what she likes most, what her favorite color is, what her favorite perfume is, etc. Even her clothing has a lot to do with the preparation of the atmosphere.

In my over forty years of marriage, and serving as pastor and marriage counselor, I have learned that a woman desires a romantic and creative man that can fill her needs. A woman desires a man who can be soft, tender, and sensual. She appreciates gentle caresses, loving words, and soft, yet passionate kisses. A man, on the other hand, wants to get right to the physical act of making love. Keep in mind that satisfying love-making does not take place if the atmosphere has not been prepared.

The atmosphere is developed in tune with the woman whom one is in love with. In addition, the atmosphere is transformed in proportion to what has been invested in the life of a person prior to the moment of making love. Atmosphere can be compared to a symphony in which many instruments are needed in order to capture the real sense of beauty in the music. In the same way, a romantic atmosphere requires different elements of the bedroom that will allow the couple to "hear" the beautiful symphony of love.

Men are the directors of the orchestra and lead the symphony in the bedroom. They control the tone and rhythm, as well as the atmosphere, to the point of filling their wife's heart with what it takes for her to give of herself completely. However, the romantic atmosphere is not reserved only for the bedroom. A romantic atmosphere can be set anywhere, anytime, and in any manner.

Most often, men are the ones who create the place and the time for romance. They are the ones who hold the keys to their wife's heart. The important aspect is being creative in setting or preparing the mood. At the same time, it is also quite acceptable for women to set the mood for a romantic evening as they are also very creative. Many times, they want to demonstrate to their husbands that they too, can show initiative when it comes to being romantic and can be on the giving as well as the receiving end. In fact, they can give even more than what they receive.

It is great that they can show this aspect of romance. It is even possible that men can learn a lot from them. Why do I say this? Because most women are much more sensitive than men; look at what I mean:

- ❑ Women are sensitive; men are insensitive.
- ❑ Women are affectionate; men find it difficult to show affection.
- ❑ Women are soft; men are rough.
- ❑ Women are simple; men are difficult.
- ❑ Women seek love; men seek sexual intercourse.
- ❑ Women show their emotions; men hide their emotions.
- ❑ Women seek understanding; men are unperceptive.

Men need to understand what their wives' truly desire from them: to be sensible, affectionate, soft, simple, loving, demonstrate emotions, and understand them at a deeper level. Most often, wives look for their husband's emotional support, protection, and respect. Many of these needs are met by maintaining a romantic atmosphere throughout their relationship.

The Issue with Women

Apart from being sensitive, women often demonstrate a strength that is quite different from that of their husbands. They can be wise or they can be stubborn, a trait that can cause much more harm than the physical strength of a man. Woman, you should allow your husband to plan and exercise creative ideas in the bedroom. Let your husband learn how to prepare the atmosphere, and how to create a romantic and pleasant night for both to enjoy. If your husband doesn't know how, help him through demonstration. Remember that most men do not instinctively know how to be romantic, much less loving. So...

- ❏ Be sensitive, not insensitive.
- ❏ Be understanding, not unperceptive.
- ❏ Be patient, not impatient.
- ❏ Be loving, not spiteful.
- ❏ Be someone who can demonstrate to her husband that he is a great man.
- ❏ Be someone who can understand him.

When a wife allows the husband to control the sexual act, bringing her to a full climax, this will bring about a transformation regarding intimacy in the husband's mind. A husband seeks approval from his wife, but if the wife undermines him with verbal negativity, he will see the bedroom quite differently. Women don't look for excuses for not making love, but rather learn to use those moments for enjoyment and allow for new dimensions in both of their lives.

THE PLANNER

Men become planners of the atmosphere. This is much like planning a party in which you need to decorate a space with balloons, prepare the music, food, and gifts. The same is true when planning time with your spouse. It may not always be appropriate to go to extremes and fill the room with balloons, but adding music, candles or even a gift for the special person you love can be very helpful. The atmosphere represents the quality of investment in the romance that a couple shares in order for the relationship to last a lifetime.

There will be times when preparing the atmosphere is not possible, so on those occasions, the atmosphere can be prepared through what we say. Words have much influence in preparing for special moments. For example: a husband can't tell his wife over and over again how much he loves her without expressing other words that will arouse her. It is very important to express one's love by adding more than one expression. Some examples are: "I love you," "I adore you," "you're my one true love," "you're all mine," "you're sweeter than honey," "you are so beautiful," "you mean everything to me," just to name a few. King Solomon expressed it beautifully in Songs of Songs 4:11: *"Your lips are as sweet as nectar, my bride. Honey and milk are under your tongue. Your clothes are scented like the cedars of Lebanon."*

In addition to being a poet, Solomon was also a romantic at heart. He knew how to reach a woman's heart by calling her "beautiful" and "my friend". However, love is demonstrated not only with words, but also through actions. Love is not only heard but can be seen as well. Love is also a verb that is expressed in action.

One of men's weaknesses is that they do not know how to demonstrate love through their actions. Most men think of their sexual desires while women want to be loved by the man she is in love with. The woman waits for him to be tender, loving, respectful, and sensitive to her needs. When a man is able to fulfill his wife's heart that way, she will give herself completely to her husband. That is what King Solomon teaches in Proverbs 4:8: *"Cherish her, and she will exalt you; embrace her, and she will honor you."*

In other words, a man needs to place his wife on a pedestal so that she will respond by doing the same for her husband. The wife must receive love first from her husband before the husband receives her love. King Solomon was wise with his wives. He knew how to reach their hearts and was able to conquer them in a romantic atmosphere. So, since the man is not by nature creative or romantic in expressing his love, intimacy is often limited through his lack of actions. Men must learn to understand their wives needs, desires, tastes, dreams, and what gives them pleasure. Men need to understand the depth of their princess's heart in order to establish their kingdom.

In a marital relationship, the husband should be the planner, the engineer, and the head of the relationship. He determines the beginning and end of each stage in the relationship. This means that the husband should be creative in his approach to winning his wife in all activities related to the relationship. A man should have a plan, a design, and ideas of what he is going to do every time he wants to get close to her. For example, if he wants to take her to the movies to see an action or war film, he would have to win her over since she would most likely prefer a romantic movie. He would plan the presentation from the beginning to the end, so that she will say yes.

The goal here is that there be a great plan for both to enjoy so that it will benefit the couple.

A woman wants a man who knows how to continually fulfill her heart with surprises. When a man is not prepared, he is indicating that he is not very sure about what he wants to do. Most men are not good planners, they lack creativity, and they do not know how to win a woman's heart. Many believe that their wife will merely follow them to the end of the world with a smile on their face. It is not like that!

IMAGINATION

Be creative, use imagination and explore ways that will lead to an unforgettable evening. It is not enough to just go to bed and wait to see if something will or not will happen. Keep in mind that there is a lot of healthy, moral material that can help a man be creative in the bedroom or any other place, in order to experience an unforgettable, out of this world evening.

Don't be afraid to look for healthy ideas that can enrich your sex life as well as your personal relationship. Men don't be boring, lazy, or afraid to explore. I can assure you that your relationship will never be the same when you use your imagination. I certainly don't encourage you to explore pornography or delve in sexual immorality. I am rather suggesting that you visit a bookstore and explore Christian books that will educate and enrich your marriage by exploring healthy and wholesome ways to strengthen the sexual appetite within the relationship and grow a good marriage.

THE OPPORTUNITY

Many intimate and romantic times occur whenever an opportunity presents itself. The sexual act does not always necessarily go according to plan. One day, as I was talking with my dad about his sexual relationship with my mom, I asked:

"How is the sexual relationship between you and mom?

Somewhat discouraged, my dad answered: "Every Friday night, when I suggest the idea to her, she remarkably has a headache that lasts all weekend."

Apparently, my poor old dad had not planned this activity well by not being creative or imaginative in the process. So, I helped him with a little advice of my own:

"It does not always have to be on weekends that you make love; sometimes it takes place when the opportunity presents itself," I said.

Then, I told him to try giving mom an aspirin for her headache, in the anticipation that there really was no headache. That would then give him the green light to carry her off to the bedroom. My dad's face lit up with such a smile that day! But then he asked:

"Son, what if it doesn't work and your mom takes the aspirin?"

"It's really very easy, dad. You have the entire week to plan your surprise," I replied. "Just find the opportunity, create the atmosphere, plan the moment, use your imagination and enjoy yourself with the wife of your youth."

My parents were eighty-five years old at the time of this writing. The passion and intimacy between them endured until my mother passed away.

THE MIND

Imagination begins in the mind, not the heart. The mind is the place where everything begins. It's the warehouse where each idea is stored. The mind is the center of creativity where beautiful ideas are born about how to build and strengthen the beauty of marriage. On the other hand, the mind is also a battlefield where wars take place, more than anywhere else in the body. The mind is where the enemy constantly attacks to destroy thoughts and ideas that will feed the marriage relationship.

The enemy does not want you to be creative, he doesn't want you to be a planner, or even be happy. Nor does he want a couple to look for romantic and intimate ways to enjoy each other's sexual relationship. He will do everything possible to pollute the mind which leads to perversion in a marriage, injecting reprobate ideas capable of ruining and destroying the marriage. Paul wrote:

> "Don't copy the behavior and customs of this world, but let God transform you into a new person by changing the way you think. Then you will learn to know God's will for you, which is good and pleasing and perfect."
>
> **(ROMANS 12:2)**

THE HEART OF MEN

I want to focus first on the heart of men and then we will talk about the heart of women. By nature, a man's heart is usually much harder than that of a woman. Men always seek logic in everything. They may try to understand the woman's heart but are unable due to hardness and immaturity. Most of a man's intentions towards his spouse may be good, but his actions show otherwise. Proverbs 16:9 says: *"We can make our plans, but the LORD determines our steps."*

Men tend to seek their own interests, what benefits them, and what comes easy without sacrifice. It is difficult for men to be sensitive to the needs of their wives because their hearts work quite differently from theirs. Men need to learn to give their heart and soul to their wives completely. I am not referring to something spiritual, but rather to a physical, emotional commitment with affection and understanding.

One of the problems that Raquel and I see quite often in our counseling sessions is that women feel that their husbands do not understand them. It is not that they do not understand them, but rather that they just do not understand a woman's heart. How do we come to this realization? Through the fact that not all men are romantic, sensitive, loving or understanding. What's more, they are not looking at their wife's heart, but rather at their unclothed body and physical appearance.

THE HEART OF WOMEN

Most women have a heart that is noble, soft, sensitive, and full of emotions. A woman's heart is bigger than a man's; not physically, but in function. Consider the following:

DISTINCTIVE QUALITIES	
HEART OF MEN	**HEART OF WOMEN**
• Hard	• Soft
• Proud	• Humble
• Unperceptive	• Understanding

• Insensitive	• Sensitive
• Spiteful	• Forgiving

Of course, not all men are like this, but many are. The conflict that we often see in our counseling sessions is the colliding of two hearts in the moment when he wants to do something in the bedroom that may be of no interest to her. This results in discomfort, tension, and insecurity in sexual intimacy, with only one of the two being satisfied with the sexual act. Two hearts have to be in the same frame of mind in order satisfy each other.

In the next chapter, you will learn how to get to know your spouse more intimately.

CHAPTER 2

KNOW YOUR SPOUSE

> **"I can see what they are doing, and I know what they are thinking."**
>
> ISAIAH 66:18

How well do you know your spouse? During the decades that Raquel and I have been involved in marriage counseling, we have found that many of the couples we counsel do not know each other very well. In virtually every marriage conference we conduct each year, we hand out a questionnaire with nine questions about how well each one knows his or her spouse. Most participants fail answering in over half of the questions. I am making these questions available here for you to answer to the best of your ability. If possible, answer them together with your spouse so that you can both confirm the extent to which you know each other:

1. What is your spouse's favorite color?
2. What is your spouse's favorite food?
3. What is the brand of your spouse's perfume or cologne?

4. What are your spouse's greatest fears?
5. What is your spouse's waist size?
6. What is your spouse's favorite movie?
7. What location in the world would your spouse like to visit one day?
8. What food does your spouse least like?
9. What are your spouse's goals?

In performing this exercise, a couple may come to realize that they do not know each other as well as they may have thought. In the event that they think they do know each other, that knowledge can still be very limited. I refer to this as outer knowledge, as opposed to inner knowledge. What is the difference? Well, allow me to explain in detail.

Exterior knowledge: Exterior knowledge is based on regular daily life activities such as work, home, dinner, and rest and then starting all over again. In essence, this knowledge involves our repeated daily tasks.

Inner knowledge: Inner knowledge refers to something deep within us, including our desires, dreams, emotions, fears, failures, and victories. These are expressed from the depth of the heart, not merely through logical thinking with our minds. Matthew 12:34 says: *"Whatever is in your heart determines what you say."* So, to know your spouse well, you must know her heart, not just her acts. I will give you a small example:

Years ago, Raquel and I were sitting together in our living room. Our two children were asleep and Raquel suggested that we lay down next to the fireplace. Her plan was to get to know me better than she already knew me. So, I laid my head on her lap, and as she stroked my head, I soon began to feel relaxed. Then she asked me, "Honey, tell me what your greatest fears are? What are your dreams and goals in life?" I immediately realized that she was reaching deep into my heart, not my mind. Without thinking, words began to just flow out of me that I had never expressed to anyone before, not even to her. It was an incredibly pleasant moment for both of us. For me, because I was able to confide in the woman who is the love of my life; for her, because it allowed her to know me in a much deeper way.

THE WEAKNESS OF MEN

It is difficult for a man to express his emotions and fears to just anyone, but especially to a woman, since that would be a demonstration of weakness. In general, men prefer to show their strengths, not their weaknesses, as well as their security, certainly not their insecurities. For a man to express his emotions to his wife, he must be very much in love.

Men that come from a Hispanic background are in general considered to be "machista" chauvinist, a word that speaks to the arrogant attitude of men regarding women in general. A real man, however, is not *chauvinist*, but rather *manly*, when he is hard-working, diligent, courageous, and firm. This is why men do not easily express or make known their feelings. To do so would be a show of weakness.

Everyone has heard at some time the expression "real men don't cry." On the other hand, another expression indicates just the opposite: "A man who cries is more of a man than one who doesn't." Despite the fact that men can often be abrupt, strong, and masculine in order to demonstrate their manliness, the reality is that they are often just soft, cuddly, timid, and fearful of the unknown. Even so, they will not show their emotions so as to not lose their manly status.

15

THE WEAKNESS OF WOMEN

Now, let's analyze the female weakness. Aside from the positive characteristics of their beauty and sensitivity in relationships, women have several weaknesses. They may be strong in character, but insecure in other ways. They can be sensitive, yet strongly opinionated.

A woman wants a man to assure her that she is beautiful in every aspect. This builds her self-esteem and strengthens her confidence. A woman desires to receive affirmations from her husband which allows her to feel secure and safe, knowing that she is loved.

A woman also needs to know that her husband is not setting his sights on other women. I am not talking about jealousy, but rather to the fact that most women pay more attention and care to the marriage than men. This is not a bad thing but it can lead to a physical distancing in the marriage if a woman is very demanding and overly protective of her husband. Naturally, there is a need for balance, a strong line of communication, and a healthy relationship, in which neither feels insecure or uncomfortable.

A husband needs to demonstrate to his wife, through behavior and actions, that she is the only one for him. If a man is too open and expressive with other women, his wife will feel insecure, and therefore, becomes demanding and overly protective of the relationship.

WHEN A HUSBAND GIVES OF HIMSELF

When a husband gives of himself to his wife, he must do so completely. This is quite like the moment when we surrender our lives to Jesus Christ; we do so in spirit, soul, and body.

The Bible teaches that in a marriage, a man and a woman become one flesh. Consequently, there must never be any secrets between them, as both have completely given of themselves to each other. This reveals the importance of knowing each other deeply. However, there are men who do not allow their wives to have access codes to their cell phones, computers or to their bank accounts. The impression they give is that they have something to hide.

Total surrender in a marriage is evident when two people give of themselves completely to one another; when they share access codes, money, cars, and even the most intimate secrets of their life. Most men give of themselves to their wife, but with conditions and secrets, wanting the freedom to go out with friends any time they want. It is easy to understand why divorce rates have increased worldwide when men are insincere in keeping their marriage vows, when they avoid being open and honest with their wives, and when they do not know each other intimately.

It could be easily assumed that a couple knows each other well because they have five children and have been married for twenty or more years; that, however, is not necessarily true. The reality is that many couples live together only as roommates, not as husband and wife. They live a lackluster life with very little communication and even less understanding. They are friends, but not lovers. They live in the same house, but sleep apart. They have a house, but not a home. They have a sexual relationship, but they never make love.

They have children, but they are not a family. They may both have jobs, but they keep separate financial accounts.

WHEN A WOMAN GIVES OF HERSELF

When a woman gives of herself, she does so completely. Unlike a man, she looks for a relationship that will last forever, one that is amazing, and certainly without surprises. Most women are much more sensitive than men, which makes their commitment much deeper than that of a man's.

Most women are devoted to the marriage vows. Her entire life is devoted to demonstrating to her husband, and to the world, that she is madly in love with him. A woman does not compare her husband with another because for her, he is the only one. She is not flirtatious with other men, nor does she desire them because there's only one man exists for her, and that is her husband. When a woman gives of herself to her husband, it is forever; there will be no other man. In most cases, her thinking is: "There is no way that this man will ever fail me or abandon me." When a woman gives of herself, it is for a lifetime.

KNOWING EACH OTHER BETTER

The Bible says in Isaiah 66:18, *"I can see what they are doing, and I know what they are thinking."* In your case, you may know the works of your spouse, but not their thoughts. To get to know your spouse's thoughts, you need to know their heart; and to know their heart, you must be in love. Love is the key to a spouse's heart, because without love, one will never be able to truly know their spouse.

It is very important that you truly get to know your spouse in such a way that even if you're apart, for reasons out of your control, trust will always keep you two knit together. To know the one to whom you promised to be with forever, you must understand that it is not only about knowing him or her deeply, but it's also about acting, investing, depositing, and even sacrificing yourself on their behalf. You have to fulfill your spouse's desires in order to demonstrate a lasting love that is genuine and true.

It is one thing to know another's thoughts and quite another to act on what you know. The word to "know" means to understand, to foresee, to anticipate, to experience; it is discovering through the exercise of one's intellectual faculties the nature, qualities, and relations of things. So, through your faculties you should come to know the qualities of your spouse and connect them with yours in order to have a long and healthy marriage.

Raquel and I are very different in many ways. I am from Costa Rica, and she is Mexican American so our customs greatly differ. For example, foods from Costa Rica are much more tropical in taste and flavor while Raquel prefers more Americanized foods. I am more acclimated to humid tropical weather while she prefers dry weather. We know each other's weaknesses as well as each other's strengths. This took time to adjust in our relationship throughout our early years in marriage but through our love for each other, we learned to accept and manage customs and traditions well.

When we got married, we pledged our vows and promised to love each other until death do us part. If we are to live together for the rest of our lives and keep that promise, we must learn to know and understand each other in a deeper way. We need to know what makes each other upset, what turns us on, as well as what turns us off; our likes as well as our dislikes. We need to know each other's dreams, goals, desires, and achievements, as well as our strengths and weaknesses. Furthermore, we should know who our friends are, and who our enemies are, what our past was like and what the future holds for us.

Over the years, we have not only learned to accept the differences between us, we have also seen a radical transformation in who we are. Our tastes have changed, our desires are different, and even our dreams have changed. Yet we have learned to know each other so much more during the process of change in our lifetime together.

When a couple knows and appreciates each other's heart deeply, it will be difficult to break the bonds of love that God has brought about through their coming together as one. You will never stop learning something new from your spouse because there will be changes throughout the years, and in the process, there will be countless new things to learn about your spouse. My deepest longing for Raquel and I is that we grow old together... and we still have many more years to go!

HOW TO STRENGTHEN COMMUNICATION

Communication in marriage is one of the main building blocks for a healthy marriage. Still, it is the ingredient least used by married couples, and most marital problems occur due to a lack of good communication. By nature, a man assumes that the woman has everything under control. On the other hand, the woman thinks that the man, as head of the home, should have everything in order. At the end of the day, the two realize that nothing was done about a matter or a situation, and then engage in a disagreement where nothing is settled because neither one wants to take responsibility.

Communication is essential to keeping order in the relationship and to maintain intimacy. It is a resource that helps produce results and brings solutions to any situation. Below, I present a series of issues where there should be good communication between you and your spouse:

Communicate...
- ❏ When making love
- ❏ When paying bills
- ❏ When plans change
- ❏ In regard to time and work
- ❏ When performing home chores
- ❏ When dealing with finances
- ❏ When discussing the children
- ❏ When discussing investments or large purchases
- ❏ When discussing the vision and future plans
- ❏ When planning vacations or time off

I could write a long list of key aspects for maintaining good communication, which unfortunately does not exist in most marriages. My intent here is to help you and your spouse strengthen the lines of communication in your marriage. First of all, make a list of important items that need attention. Take one item per day and talk about it for ten to fifteen minutes without any arguments. To that end, do the following:

1. Talk about the problems or the situation at hand.
2. Look for a solution and agree to it together.
3. Pray together when you are finished discussing the matter.

Now, let's take a look at an example of how to strengthen communication in a marriage:

PROBLEM: Insecurity and Lack of Privacy

Woman: I feel as if you don't love me. I don't feel any affection or endearment.

Man: You *know* that I love you. What more do you expect from me?

Woman: It's just that you don't touch me anymore. You're always tired and you spend most of your time with your friends or watching television. I want to feel your love and your affection. I don't want to have to think that there might be someone else.

SOLUTION: Response to communication

Man: Please forgive me. I didn't know you felt that way. I promise that I won't spend so much time with my friends so that I can be with you more. I'll do my best to show you how much I love you by being more affectionate every day. I didn't realize you felt this way.

PRAYER: For help

Lord, forgive me for my selfish behavior and for being insensitive to my wife's needs. Help me, Lord, to be a better man every day and to watch over her heart. Amen.

Without creating upheaval in a teapot, keep in mind that this should not take more than ten or fifteen minutes. This exercise not only helps to solve problems, but it also opens the lines of communication in which the time spent talking with each other can grow from ten minutes to an hour or more. Another idea would be to go on a romantic date and set a specific topic of conversation to keep the evening from becoming boring. It's important to not talk about problems or the children on a romantic date. Instead, talk about love, dreams, aspirations, and the things you both enjoy doing. Make every effort to create a pleasant, romantic atmosphere.

BUILDING A STRONG RELATIONSHIP

I often say that a marriage is like a garden that must be continually cultivated and tended to. In a relationship, one must find new ways to nourish and keep it from drying up and becoming boring. This is where creativity, the ability to build and nurture the unity between husband and wife, comes into play. A relationship is not necessarily built on gifts, taking trips or romantic dates. Rather, a relationship is built over time through communication, listening, understanding, imagination, and devotion.

Understanding: A relationship is formed by two individuals who deeply love each other, but do not necessarily understand one another. Part of building a strong relationship is getting to know and understand each other, and that involves building on each other's strengths while growing the marriage. It is common for both partners to have come from different backgrounds, and the likes, ideas, and feelings may also be different. These are factors that need to be understood in order to build the relationship, as always, through love and understanding.

Sensitivity: Another aspect in the building of a relationship is sensitivity in all areas, whether it be physical, emotional, intellectual, or spiritual. It is critical to learn to discern between the negative and the positive, the likes and dislikes. Sensitivity is connected to the emotions, to feelings and the heart, which means that a great part of healthy relationships are established in these areas. Love is a feeling that forms in the heart. With that said, if in a relationship these feelings and emotions do not exist, it is possible that love doesn't exist either.

The Bible tells us the following: *"A cheerful heart is good medicine, but a broken spirit aps a person's strength."* (Proverbs 17:22)

A joyful heart can be seen in these ways:

- ❏ The recognition of the truth through sensitivity to the person you love the most.
- ❏ The solution of a marital conflict by being sincere at heart.
- ❏ The forgiveness that comes from being sensitive to another person's pain.
- ❏ The love that develops by being sensitive to a partner's needs.
- ❏ The enjoyment of intimacy by being sensitive to a loved one.

Later in the book, chapter six, we will look further into the area of sensitivity.

CHAPTER 3

ENJOY THE MOMENT

> **"Has anyone planted a vineyard and not begun to enjoy it?"**
>
> DEUTERONOMY 20:6 (NIV)

One of the steps of love is to enjoy the union between a husband and wife. The word 'enjoy' is a synonym of savor, have fun, rejoice, contentment, be glad, delight and be happy. For me, being married is not just a matter of being close to my wife, but it is *truly* enjoying her company. Couples need to take advantage of all the time they can spend together and enjoy each other at every opportunity, filled with the delight of being together. Mutual enjoyment always seeks the opportunity to nurture oneness.

Marriage is much like a garden that can become extravagant, delicate and beautiful, all of which takes time to develop and maintain. The soil must be prepared and the weeds kept back. Then flowers must be planted, watered, and properly pruned while awaiting to see their beauty in full bloom. During the process of cultivation, one needs to enjoy the process of the labor. Understand

25

that each new day in a marriage is different from the one before. Each moment has its unique demands, needs, faults, weaknesses, desires, and pleasures. Nevertheless, we must never allow the negative aspects of life to drown out the positive ones. That is why it is very important that we enjoy every single moment with our spouse.

In my case, I want Raquel to be at my side, not only in my failures, but also in my victories. I also want to be by her side to enjoy every moment with her because together, we are creating tomorrow's memories and those memories will in turn, become the stories that we share with our children and our grandchildren. I really like what Moses tells us in Deuteronomy 20:6 (NIV): *"Has anyone planted a vineyard and not begun to enjoy it? Let him go home, or he may die in battle and someone else enjoy it."* I must be the husband who enjoys a full life with my wife so that no other man would take that place in her life.

The Bible says that we do not know what *"life will be like tomorrow"* (James 4:14). That means that we should live today as if it were our very last day, enjoying every moment, every breath, every touch, and every opportunity that we have with our spouse.

DON'T WASTE YOUR TIME ARGUING

Don't waste your time arguing and constantly fighting with each other. Don't waste a single day not talking with each other because nobody knows what tomorrow will bring. Enjoy each moment and bask in the pleasure of being with the person you love the most.
I understand that there will be difficult times in any marriage. However, I would rather spend my time solving the problem than

doing nothing, because the sooner the conflict can be resolved, the sooner the moment can be enjoyed.

Now returning to the matter of creativity, keep in mind the following: "Marriage is what we allow it to be." If you want a boring marriage, you will have a boring marriage. If you want a healthy marriage, you will have a healthy marriage. In a boring marriage one simply has to do nothing; there is nothing to invest, and no need to try hard at anything. Furthermore, there is no need to demonstrate an interest in the other person. However, in order to have a healthy marriage, one needs to invest love, time, strength, creativity, feelings, and dream together.

In many instances, the environment should be created, set the stage for a moment of laughter, dedicate time for the memories, and enjoy past moments that have been experienced. Couples should enjoy each moment especially when difficult times arise. Learn to lean into one another for support when facing crisis in the relationship. Couples need to learn to enjoy life on rainy days as well as during hot blistering times, whether there is enough money or not, whether they sleep on the floor or on a nice soft bed, whether they have a car or have to walk because there is no transportation. Remember the promise you each made to each other when you got married. In my case, I promised Raquel the following: "I, David, take you Raquel, to be my lawfully wedded wife so that the two of us can be one from this day forward, for better or for worse, in sickness or in health, for richer or poorer, to care for you and love you, until death do us part."

These were the vows that Raquel and I took on September 4, 1982. While reviewing those vows recently, we reminded ourselves that we made a promise to enjoy every moment together: in good times as well as in times of difficulty and adversity, in sickness or in health, for richer or poorer, and during our forty plus years of marriage, we have definitely experienced the challenges. The key, and very important aspect of a marriage, is that a couple enjoy every moment together, both in pleasant times as well as in unpleasant times, because the most significant aspect of things that come our way in life is facing it together.

ENJOY THE MOMENT

Every three months Raquel and I make every effort to have a weekend together that is out of our ordinary routine. It is an effort because there is a great demand for our time in ministry. And because our calling is so very important to us, it can be easy to forget to set time apart for us to enjoy.

We have many assignments as we travel to different parts the world hosting marriage conferences, we pastored a congregation for twenty-seven years, I served as a Police Chaplain in our city for eighteen years, and I make time to write books that can help strengthen marriages; so while having such busy schedules and all, we had to learn to be very creative with balancing our family life. Most importantly, we dedicate family time to spend with our children and grandchildren. I strongly believe that throughout the years, Raquel and I have deserved to spend those weekends together without having to think about ministry or the demands of life.

From time to time, we and our grown adult children, their spouses, and our grandchildren travel together for family vacations. Still then, Raquel and I manage to set time aside to spend our special moments together. Enjoying marriage is an indication of a couple in love while getting along with each other. It's important to note that when a loving couple invests in each other's lives their marriage is strengthened and enriched as time passes. Couples need to find time to be alone together for romantic moments by either taking a walk, going on a picnic or just holding hands while walking through a park. It can even be romantic to share ordinary household chores, like cleaning the house, cooking, washing...and even making love in the living room when they are alone!

Couples need to be creative and enjoy every moment together. Couples should not let the day go by without laughing or sharing intimate moments together. Remember love *"does not rejoice about injustice but rejoices whenever the truth wins out. Love never gives up, never loses faith, is always hopeful, and endures through every circumstance."* (1 Corinthians 13:6-7)

In the oneness of a marriage, part of the growth and development of each spouse is found in being patient with each other, waiting on each other, bearing each other's burdens and believing in each other. So even when we are enduring, we can enjoy the moment. What does James tell us in his epistle? *"When troubles of any kind come your way, consider it an opportunity for great joy"* (James 1:2). Notice that joy is part of the word "enjoy". So, enjoy each moment and learn from the experience, because those times will be the ones that create lasting memories for the future.

TREASURE WHAT YOU HAVE

On one occasion, my mother-in-love revealed a great truth to me. She said, "David, when I die, I don't want flowers at my funeral."

"Why not?" I asked.

"Because I won't be able to enjoy them from the grave," she replied. "I'd much rather receive flowers now while I'm alive, than tomorrow after I'm dead."

Wow... That is a great truth! I want to give Raquel all my love now while I have her close to me. Why wait until it's too late?

Every day comes at a cost, so learn to treasure what you have. Remember your commitment, and enjoy every moment that you share together. To place value in what you have, you will need to invest time, energy and commitment. When you take the time to invest in what you love, it's because you truly believe in it. In believing what you've established within your marriage, then there is a continued interest in investing all of you in order to achieve the end result of a better, happier, and more fulfilling marriage!

If a husband is unfaithful to his wife, the result will be great harm to both partners. If the woman is acting foolish and angry, the result of her attitude will cause great harm to both as well. When a husband-and-wife love and respect each other, the result will be a happy and healthy marriage. An important key to remember is this: The final result of a healthy marriage will be determined by the size of one's investment into it.

LEARN TO INVEST

When I talk about investing, I do not mean the investing of money, but rather of time. A good investment will always produce a good profit. The more you invest in the marriage, the foundation of the relationship will grow stronger. Both husband and wife should set aside time away from children, work, and church. Being too busy for each other is always a dangerous sign. While raising children, keep in mind that the marriage relationship itself, came before the family. Don't allow the children to think that they must have your undivided attention one hundred percent of the time. Keep schedules both daily and weekly, setting aside time for household responsibilities, the care of children, and the marriage relationship.

Look for ways to have fun, such as romantic walks on the beach, and perhaps drawing hearts on the sand with your names in them. Visit local parks with a picnic basket or snacks to share under a tree. It's even fun to carve out your initials on a tree trunk with your anniversary date beneath. Use your God-given creativity to fill your days and nights with love.

BE CREATIVE

Let go of your traditional way of thinking and be creative in your marriage! Look for new places to visit, stretching out toward new horizons. Take walks at night, and not just during the day; try taking the bus together to a destination and leave the car at home. These are just a few creative ideas that will strengthen the bonds of your marriage. Remember that you are best friends with your spouse, and friends know how to enjoy every moment. One idea may be to double-date with other couples, learning new ideas from them. These may include new styles, strategies, places to visit, restaurants to try out, and even be creative with your personal appearance.

Creativity is a never-ending resource that will sharpen great ideas on romance and intimacy. Also, learn to be creative in your private moments by making love in various rooms throughout the house, in a hotel or even in another city when possible. Be ready and willing to take advantage of the endless possibilities because those special moments you create will be a wondrous adventure in your married life.

KNOW HOW TO PLAN THE FAMILY

From the very beginning, God's purpose for His creation was to replenish itself in all its fullness. We are told in Genesis that God created man, He looked and said it was not good that man should be alone. So, he created woman to be his companion: *"Then God blessed them and said, "Be fruitful and multiply. Fill the earth and govern it. Reign over the fish in the sea, the birds in the sky, and all the animals that scurry along the ground."* (Genesis 1:28)

God's plan for Adam and Eve was to multiply and fill the earth. Today, that multiplication is what we call family. While the family is a major part of a marriage, the problem is that not everyone plans for their own family. A marriage relationship needs to be solid enough to support a family. A great number of divorces today occur because the family is not planned properly. If there is no initial family planning and structure during the early stages of the marriage, the foundation and strength in the relationship may suffer consequences later on. When children begin to arrive, romance and communication fades away. The dynamics of friendship in the marriage changes, and with it begins the loss of respect and attention for each other; the focus is now on the family and not on the marriage itself. Raquel and I always encourage new couples who plan on marrying each other to spend at least two to three years of togetherness before planning a family.

ENJOY YOUR CHILDREN

Once the family is planned, and children are added, it is time to enjoy the growing process of a family. Children are a gift from the Lord, but they are also a high demand on one's time and energy. Learn how to give them the time they need so that the two of you can later enjoy a quiet, romantic moment together. One always has to try to balance the hours of each day to allow time to enjoy each other.

One of the most common mistakes in a marriage is to put the children first ahead of the couple themselves. The marriage should always come first, and children second. Here are some guidelines to follow:

- ❏ Know how to invest adequate time with your children, so that as a couple you can enjoy time alone with each other.
- ❏ Know how to balance your time (Ecclesiastes 3:1).
- ❏ Teach your children to respect mom and dad's alone time (Proverbs 6:20).
- ❏ Guide your children on the right path (Proverbs 22:6).
- ❏ Take one day each week for family time.
- ❏ Dad, find time to be alone with your children (Proverbs 4:1).
- ❏ Mom, find time to be alone with your children (Proverbs 1:8).

As you take the time to practice these points, you will start to see how much it will help you to not only raise your children, but also to truly enjoy them.

CHAPTER 4

BE ROMANTIC

> **"Let me see your face; let me hear your voice. For your voice is pleasant, and your face is lovely."**
>
> **SONG OF SOLOMON 2:14**

It has been said that romance is the flame of love. My question would be "What is the definition of romance?" In reality, romance can mean something completely different to different people. For example, when a man opens a car door for his wife, some women will see that as being romantic. Others, however, see it simply an act of courtesy. When a man buys flowers for his wife on any ordinary day, she can see it as a romantic gesture; on the other hand, another woman may think that there is something the man wants. The dictionary can provide more information regarding other meanings of the words romantic and romance:

❑ Romance: 1) a literary work of fiction. 2) A casual, passing love relationship.

- ❑ Romanticism: The state or quality of being romantic, sentimental.
- ❑ Romantic: Sentimental, generous and an idealized view of reality.

I hope these definitions provide a little more understanding of what the word "romantic" can mean. Having a knowledge of these meanings can enable you to become a romantic person as well as how to continue to be romantic.

I can understand that for many individuals, being romantic does not come easily, perhaps because they were raised in an environment where romance was not regularly or easily evident. Perhaps one's parents did not show affection in public, much less be romantic in front of others. Nevertheless, all of that is open to change. One of the first and most important ways to be romantic would be to know your spouse well by discovering their tastes, understanding their feelings, sharing their desires and fulfilling their fantasies; but most of all, dedicating time to explore your spouse's heart, mind and soul.

Romance comes in many shapes and sizes. In my case, I keep in mind that Raquel loves listening to romantic music when we are together. One of our favorite songs is "Toda Una Vida" ("A Whole Life" in Spanish), which I dedicated to her on the eve before our wedding. I remember the night that two of my friends strummed their guitars as I serenaded her through the window of her bedroom. These are the translated words of the song:

> I will be with you for a lifetime
> And nothing else matters,
> It doesn't matter where or how, but near you always.
> I will spend a lifetime pampering you,
> I will take care of you like I care for myself,

I will live for you.
I won't get tired of telling you,
that you are the greatest part of my life.
You are my joy, my happiness, and my greatest love!

I will be with you for a lifetime,
And nothing else matters,
It doesn't matter where or how, but near you always.

Since then, of course, I have learned to explain the idea of romanticism in other ways. At one of our United in Love Marriage conferences, I was asked, "How can a person remain romantic?" My reply was simple and with another question: "How does a person stay in good physical shape?" To do that, most people would join a gym to train and keep their body in shape. The same idea holds true for staying romantic, and that is by finding ways to train and exercise your romantic side. The book Song of Solomon in the Bible provides a good example: *"Let me see your face; let me hear your voice. For your voice is pleasant, and your face is lovely."* (Song of Solomon 2:14)

Solomon was not only a great king, but also an amazing poet who knew how to win his wives over by reaching their hearts. Men, however, do not have to be the only romantics in a relationship. Women can and should be romantic as well. Even though men may not be overly sentimental by nature, it does not mean that they do not enjoy when their wife is romantic with them. Of course, perspectives may vary from that of women, but men do enjoy romance from their spouse.

PLAN A ROMANTIC DAY

Back in January 11, 1993, while I was working for Bank of America, Raquel secretly planned an out-of-town weekend for us and kidnapped me from my office on my thirtieth birthday. She worked out all the details in advance as to how she would get me to leave work. She even spoke with my supervisor and got me to take the rest of the afternoon off without me knowing. That Friday at noon, she came to take me out to lunch. She even had a suitcase packed for the weekend in the trunk of the car.

After lunch, she blindfolded my eyes and told me not to worry about returning to work that afternoon. She had planned the perfect birthday weekend for me. She then drove me to a beautiful seaside hotel with an amazing room that overlooked the ocean. The bed had been covered with rose petals, along with a plate of chocolate covered strawberries. I won't share the rest of our intimate moments we shared but you can use your imagination! Raquel created a very romantic weekend for us to spend together, and I'll never forget it. Waking up to a delicious breakfast in bed the next morning while watching the crashing ocean waves through the window, and feeling the sea breeze caress our faces, surpassed by far that romantic weekend.

It is essential to have an adventurous spirit with a creative imagination that can fill your heart with so much love. One can learn to be romantic by watching romantic movies, reading romantic books, or just listening to the heartbeat of the one you love. Many seem to believe that courtship is the only time for romance, and that aspect of a relationship is ignored once the spouse has been won over. That is perhaps the biggest mistake one can make in the life of a marriage. The idea of romance should never be stifled because it is the spark that keeps the flame of love alive for a lifetime. Romance fuels intimacy, and it is the power of sexuality as well as the bond of love that holds two people together.

LEARN TO BE ROMANTIC

Learn to be romantic and express who you are, by how you are, by the way you speak, and even by the way you love. Romance comes in different shapes and sizes, with different tones and sounds, in different ways and expressions. Romance is not only an idea, but also an action, an expression, a way to demonstrate love for the other person in a different way each time.

Romance is a song that can take you into a deeper dimension of love. It is an action that can change your direction. When you are romantic, you become sensitive with your spouse's heart. A marriage without romance is just two friends hanging out together, and nothing else. That is why it's so important that you make time in your schedule to go for walks with your spouse. Then, while holding hands, open your hearts to each other and talk or just listen.

You don't need money to be romantic. You don't need a fancy, late-model car to be romantic. You don't even have to try hard to be romantic. What is essential is having a heart full of love and creative ideas.

THE THIEVES OF ROMNCE

What are the things that destroy a marriage? I'd like to give you a list of factors that have been destroying romance in a marriage for many decades. I call these the thieves of romance. Many married couples have allowed for the romance to die in their marriages by ignorance and a lack of priority in their spouse. Televisions are set in the bedroom to consume time watching movies and programs that do not nurture the couple's intimacy. Couples spend lots of money on the latest screen tv's, but find it difficult to invest in a romantic getaway. Married couples spend more money on having the latest cellphones, fashion trends or buy new cars. Some may have to work three jobs just to be able to pay all the debts they get into. They just can't find the time to invest in their spouse appropriately. They end up being too tired or too busy; they even use the excuse that the kids don't let them spend quality time together or that they are better off postponing romantic time for the future. Romantic dates never make it to the forefront of the relationship.

HOW TO ENJOY ROMANCE

Romance can be enjoyed in a number of different ways, either at home or away from home. Romance has nothing to do with the sexual act, but rather the sensibility and passion of sharing a pure and noble love. Romance is an emotional act that is born from within the soul. It's an emotional act. It's a passionate and motivational moment. Romance doesn't have a price; it is something spontaneous and it becomes the fuel for love. Consider the following:

- ❏ The moment of romance should be pleasant for both.
- ❏ It demands investment and creativity from both.
- ❏ It takes time and self-will.
- ❏ Romance helps prepare the atmosphere for an intimate evening.

When a couple enjoys a romantic moment together, and truly enjoy each other's company, this demonstrates a passionate and loving growth. Romance should bring pleasure, it should never be boring. Don't allow the romance killers to destroy your married life.

THE CLIMATE OF ROMANCE

Romance becomes what couple designs it to be. Romance is the moment; it's the evening climate, the perfume in the air, and the smile that welcomes the freshness and tenderness of a new day. Romance causes inner heat from within the soul, a burning fuel for the sweet moment ahead. Romance is the door to intimacy, brightness like the sun for the soul, but it's also like the soft shadows of a moonlit night.

A romantic climate is the atmosphere that permeates that unique place where two hearts come together as one, filling any void that may exist in the soul. A romantic mood is where two people choose to enjoy the special sweetness that loving words between them brings. It is that time that one takes to understand and appreciate a partner in the deepest and most intimate way possible. Romance is transformed into the loving words that you share with your spouse reaching into the depths of each other's heart.

"How beautiful you are, my darling, how beautiful! Your eyes are like doves. You are so handsome, my love, pleasing beyond words! The soft grass is our bed;"

(SONG OF SOLOMON 1:15-16)

Without a doubt, romance converts into pleasant thoughts that cross your mind to help enjoy each moment spent together.

ROMANCE IS A TWO-WAY STREET

Romanticism should not only be limited to the man in a relationship, but must also be shared by the woman. The man is generally the romance initiator, the guide, the lead; but the woman should also feel free to initiate the moment, the evening or the act. I believe that in a marriage both partners should be romantic, passionate and madly in love. Each has much to offer in the relationship.

When a wife has had a hard and busy day at work, it may be her husband who initiates romance. At other times, the wife will be the initiator of romance because the husband has had a heavy and exhausting day at work. There will also be days when both will have renewed energy and a great sexual appetite, an explosive energy of being together in a dark romantic place where the two can express themselves in a pleasant way for both. When both partners are romantic, it is much easier to keep the flame of passion burning in their relationship while keeping the garden of their love cultivated. The following are some suggestions to keep in mind:

❏ Take turns at being the initiator of romantic moments.
❏ Look for new and exciting places to go together.
❏ Surprise your partner with something romantic, such as a poem or a flower.
❏ Choose one day each week to be alone together without the children or visitors.
❏ Practice courtship without making love.

These ideas will help to stimulate the interest in loving romance, and will help to build a lasting relationship between a husband and wife.

In the next chapter, I will discuss how to keep the "flame burning" as well as the Steps of Love needed to develop and maintain a healthy marriage relationship.

"Let me see your face; let me hear your voice. For your voice is pleasant, and your face is lovely."

(SONG OF SOLOMON 2:14)

CHAPTER 5

KEEPING THE FLAME ALIVE

> **"As the fire burns the woods, and as the flame sets the mountains on fire,"**
>
> **PSALM 83:14**

The flame from a fire always brings heat to those who are surrounding it. In a marriage, the flame of passion should not only be lit when a couple is making love; the embers should also be kept ready to light the fire at any moment or in any situation that may arise.

The flame of love is kept burning through caresses, tenderness, sexual intimacy, hugs, kisses, time together, communication, and comprehension. When we deposit to our loved one what he or she needs or seeks, we are filling in any gaps that may exist in the relationship. The flame is the source of the romantic energy that exists in a couple, and it is kept burning by being sensitive at all times to one another's needs. On the other hand, when the flame goes out, any warmth between the two can be lost.

For example, when Raquel and I are counseling a married couple, and we see that there is a lack of communication or understanding between the couple, we can easily see that the flame has burned out. Even if they continue to have a sexual relationship, it does not mean that it is an act of love, but rather mere physical gratification, not real sexual intimacy.

The sexual act alone serves only to satisfy the desires of the flesh, not those of the heart. Sexual intimacy is all about entering another person's heart by expressing love intimately to the person before entering the physical part. While the act of making love should last at least thirty to forty-five minutes, the simple act of physical sex itself may take only five minutes. When the flame is lit, one does not want the moment to end because the two hearts are connected in the most intimate dimension of love making.

The flame I am referring to leads you to explore your spouse's body in a deeper dimension. This will result in a woman reaching a full orgasmic climax, causing chills throughout her entire body. In a similar way, it helps a man maintain a better erection during the intimate sexual act and he as well, will experience greater physical, pleasurable sensations.

THE FLAME IS THE FUEL

A married couple can't love without an existing flame. The flame is the fuel of an intimate moment. For example, the Holy Spirit is the fuel for the Christian believer; it is the flame of fire that moves and fills us. In much the same way, there is a flame in the heart that ignites in an intimate relationship between husband and wife.

Love can be sustained by emotions or devotion. When love is sustained by emotions, it becomes a simple desire; to care or to like. To like is not the same as to love. To like is to enjoy while to love is sacrificial. There are couples who like each other, but do not love each other, because the flame has burned out. When one loves with devotion, it is because there is a special inclination or special affection that helps to keep the flame alive.

The flame helps one to be romantic, sensitive to the needs of a spouse, and more creative in the relationship. Even more, it allows us to respect and honor the person we love the most in life. Ephesians 5:33 says: *"each man must love his wife as he loves himself, and the wife must respect her husband."*

The apostle Paul is very clear on how we should behave as a couple, and how a man should love his wife: *"For husbands, this means to love your wives, just as Christ loved the church. He gave up his life for her"* (Ephesians 5:25). So, when the flame is not lit, love transforms into like versus love, and the respect is lost in the relationship. The flame of love burns out in a marriage when:

- ❏ There is no longer mutual respect.
- ❏ There is no romance, no understanding, no communication.
- ❏ There are more excuses than caresses and neither spouse has time for the other.
- ❏ The couple sleeps in separate beds or bedrooms.
- ❏ The couple spends more time with friends than with each other.

The way to keep the flame burning is through investing time with the person you love the most. Consider the following guidelines to keep the flame burning:

- ❏ Learn to pray and have a devotional time together.
- ❏ Set aside time alone to talk and share time together.
- ❏ Learn to make love, and not just have sex.

- ❏ Be creative in intimacy.
- ❏ Express love and mutual respect.
- ❏ Learn to meet each other's needs.
- ❏ Be romantic, tender, kind, loving, and understanding.

There is nothing more beautiful than a healthy married relationship to keep the flame burning. Without that flame, romance will not be effective. This may be new and somewhat difficult for many to accept, since most parents never taught or demonstrated this kind of love life. There are many people who were never explained openly about sexual relationships because it was considered filthy or taboo in their culture.

There are very few teachings regarding this matter since no one wants to speak about something that has been considered a taboo in our culture. The enemy has contaminated the matter and has covered it with lies and vulgarity, so that the children of God do not discuss it. However, today I can tell you that what God created, regarding sexuality in the context of love, within the confines of a marriage, is beautiful and pure.

WHAT TURNS THE FLAME OFF?

Please know that watching pornography does nothing to help keep the flame burning. In reality, pornography gives way to lustful thoughts and eventually to sexual immorality. It contaminates the purity of a sexual relationship, destroying the passion of true love. In the end, pornography develops wicked thoughts, instilling a desire to experience things outside of the marriage. Pornography brings shame and guilt and can ultimately bring about separation between a husband and wife, as well as develops an unclean mind set and a perverse heart. Pornography strengthens sexual activity but weakens sexual intimacy. There is no better sexual relationship than one that is pure, clean, and free of all perversity. In Hebrews 13:4, the Bible teaches us to: *"Give honor to marriage, and remain faithful to one another in marriage. God will surely judge people who are immoral and those who commit adultery."*

In a number of older translations of the Bible, this verse says that the marriage bed should be undefiled. The word "defile"[1] means to sully, mar, spoil, to desecrate or profane something sacred. This means that the marriage bed must be a holy and honorable place before God; that is, without sin or infidelity. Fornicators and adulterers will be judged by God which leads us to understand that infidelity of any kind, represented by immorality and pornography, is not acceptable in the marriage bed.

It is critical to avoid other couples or individuals who may exert a bad influence on your life. Being around negative and pessimistic people can easily affect and make you become like them. Over time, negative people can even lead to sinful acts within the marriage. Bad influences are like an infection that, in the long run, contaminates trust, fidelity, loyalty, and even sexual intimacy. A true friend respects and cares for the unity of your marriage. A true friend seeks the well-being of the friendship that exists. On the other hand, the friend who does not consider the well-being of your marriage is not a true friend.

Set your mind to be that flame that burns every day for your spouse; the flame that will enable you to see and accept the attractiveness and beauty of your spouse. Never allow the flame of romanticism to burn out, the flame of love, the flame that will keep you burning with passion out of your love for each other.

---

[1] The word defile has the additional meaning of "to violate the chastity of (a woman)".

WHAT LIGHTS THE FLAME

The flame is lit with the match of passion, with a carbon of tenderness, or with a bit of romanticism. These are just some of the many ways to help ignite the flame in a relationship. The flame has various purposes in a relationship. First, the flame illuminates the perfect path in a marriage, and it's the light that reflects a marriage that is alive and healthy. Secondly, the flame brings a healthy warmth to the relationship and it protects the marriage against cooling off periods or boredom due to the lies and myths of this world. Thirdly, the flame keeps the atmosphere warm and comfortable, and always ready for the unexpected moment.

When there are no traces of romanticism in a marriage, or the passion has gone out of the relationship, the flame will weaken and eventually die out. It is important to be romantic and passionate in the relationship, looking for creative ways to keep the flame burning at all times. Remember that a sexual relationship is the heat from the flame, and intimacy is the manifestation or outcome of the flame. The most beautiful aspect of a healthy relationship is being able to keep the flame burning at all times, in any place, and at any time of the day. This shows that the relationship has been built on a good foundation and has a solid structure.

THE HEAT FROM THE FLAME

The flame is what warms the soul and ignites sexual desires. When one is focused on intimacy, the heat from the flame can be felt as it keeps the setting comfortable. The lack of a burning flame between spouses, however, is very easily noticed. Through their behavior, one can see that they have become dull, boring, and an insensitive couple. There is no interest in the relationship since they are selfish, foolish, void of any understanding, and they lack tenderness and comprehension. These are couples who have fallen out of love and stay in the relationship for interest but not for love. On the other hand, the flame is the evidence where two people deeply love and respect each other; it is the fruit of love and the manifestation of romance and fidelity.

THE ENJOYMENT OF THE FLAME

A flame is enjoyed when the couple is of one mind, and there are no barriers or concerns in the relationship. The enjoyment of the flame in a marriage is much like that of a delight, laying together near a fireplace on a cold and stormy night and holding a cup of hot chocolate while embracing under a blanket to keep warm. When one can enjoy the flame of romance, it is because there is an everlasting, incomprehensible love. The goal is to seek each other's total satisfaction.

In the enjoyment of the flame of love, however, there is a price to pay which includes a total sacrificial surrender. The covenant that was made at an altar before God and many witnesses, must be kept and protected. The flame is lit after the commitment is established by both. God gives us that flame after we say: "yes, I do, till death do us part." This gift from God is a symbol of unity, a covenant that is meant for the enjoyment of a new life together within God's perfect plan.

There is no excuse for a married couple to not enjoy the burning flame throughout their lifetime together. If one does not enjoy the flame in marriage, it may be because there are other factors distracting their relationship, thereby drawing them apart rather than keeping them close.

WHAT HAPPENS IF THE FLAME BURNS OUT?

When a couple comes to our office for counseling, the first thing Raquel and I look for is some background information regarding their behavior. We take a good look at the problem and the excuses that are made to justify a divorce. Quite often, the flame has burned out due to infidelity or loss of emotional connection. In other cases, however, it was extinguished merely through lack of caring, failing to give attention to love or just not showing concern for the relationship. However, neither spouse wants to assume responsibility for the cause of the flame that burned out.

A young couple came to see us after a few years of marriage with no seeming hope of staying in their relationship. According to them, they had done everything possible to be happy but without any results. There had been no sexual infidelity, no other lovers; they just did not know how to keep their flame burning for love. They had agreed to end the relationship because their love had burned out. I was not willing to accept such an excuse. The truth is that this couple had never built the necessary foundation nor received specific instructions on how to save the relationship. At once, the Lord put in my spirit an idea that I presented to them at that time:

"Do you think there is still a small drop of love in your relationship?" I asked.

They looked into each other's eyes and both responded with virtually the same response:

"Yes, but it is a very small drop, and not much more."

"Well, that is all that God needs," I replied with a smile.

I told them that their marriage did not have to end, but rather this time could be the beginning of something new that God could do in their lives. I asked them to remain apart for six months and during that time, to date once a month in a romantic setting where they could start over as very good friends. They were not to kiss, have any physical contact or intimacy. At the end of the evening, he was to take her home and say goodnight without touching her.

By the end of the third month, the couple returned to my office requesting an urgent session. They told me that during the three months of their trial separation, they could not bear to be apart. At the end of each of those three dates, they had gone to a hotel to revive the flame that they believed had burned out. During those three months they realized how much they were in love, but had not known how to keep the flame burning. That same day in my office, they renewed their vows and promised to rebuild on a new foundation and a new life in Christ. Seven months later they became parents to an adorable baby girl who transformed their lives forever.

If you think the flame has burned out in your marriage, it would be wise to find a Christian counselor to help you. Remember that nothing is impossible for God. Love must be *"As the fire burns the woods, and as the flame sets the mountains on fire."* (Psalm 83:14)

CHAPTER 6

BE SENSITIVE TO LOVE

> **"Kiss me and kiss me again, for your love is sweeter than wine."**
>
> SONG OF SOLOMON 1:2

O n many occasions the word sensitive has a weak connotation. The word "sensitive" can be defined as "having perception through the senses", which includes the expression of sentiments, or feelings. In any relationship there are positive and negative feelings, but particularly in a marriage it is very important that both husband and wife remain sensitive to each other's heart and feelings. Feelings manifest themselves in a way which *we* feel, so it is important to be sensitive to the other person's feelings.

A man, for example, may not be very sensitive to the needs of a woman, much less to her feelings. In 1 Corinthians 13, where the apostle Paul teaches on the meaning of love, he writes about the one who is sensitive in love: *"Love never gives up, never loses faith, is always hopeful, and endures through every circumstance"* (v. 7). In other words, we cannot take for granted the power behind love.

We need to keep in mind the importance of being sensitive to love. Still, sensitivity is not something one is born with, but rather is forged through the process of sacrifice. Sensitivity is revealed in the care that is taken towards the other person. In the 40 plus years of marriage, I have learned to be sensitive to Raquel's heart and feelings continuously. We have both learned to protect our hearts by careful use of our words and our actions. For example, if I said something that caused pain to her heart, that would create an emotional separation, or if I treated her in such a way that would cause her frustration, that would affect our intimacy.

My words can have the same effect as my actions. Men need to work at being more sensitive in their relationships because women live in the realm of emotions more than men. Men tend to be hard-hearted and show emotions much less than women. On the other hand, women tend to be more sensitive, tender-hearted, and more noble than that of men.

SENSITIVITY BRINGS SECURITY

A relationship cannot endure the problems of married life if one is guided solely by the mind, and not the heart. Sensitivity brings security in a marriage. Raquel once told me that what she needed from me was security. Security is the certainty, the guarantee, of my love for her. As one of the results of love, security is the lock to her heart and knowing that I would never abandon her. You can say to your spouse "I love you" but the way to demonstrate it is not through the sexual act itself but in being sensitive to your spouse's heart. Sensitivity to your spouse's heart will lead to unforgettable nights in the bedroom.

The Bible gives this perfect instruction for husbands: *"In the same way, you husbands must give honor to your wives. Treat your wife with understanding as you live together. She may be weaker than you are, but she is your equal partner in God's gift of new life."* (1 Peter 3:7)

❏ *To give honor* means to "show careful thought; not to cause inconvenience or hurt to another". In addition, the word careful in this definition can mean "anxious to protect with thought and attention". (Note: the word in the original Greek is *gnosis*, which means "knowledge")

❏ *To treat with understanding* says that I must respect and admire her as a woman for her abilities, qualities, and achievements as well as having regard for her feelings, wishes, and rights.

❏ *Weaker* does not mean unequal, but indicates that I must recognize her sensitive heart.

When we are soft, tender, loving, affectionate, kind, and respectful, we demonstrate through these actions that we are being sensitive to love. Of course, not only does a man have the responsibility to be sensitive to his wife's heart, but the woman also plays a big part in this aspect of the relationship. When we speak of "sensitivity", it is evident that men are somewhat different from women because men tend to have more of a hardened heart.

Because most men are not emotional beings, and don't generally show their emotions, most men express their emotions through silence, while most women often demonstrate emotions through their tears. Some men will demonstrate their emotions through violence and aggressiveness, due to not knowing how to control their emotions.

Men use their masculinity and strength to demonstrate their feelings, while women express their emotions with sensitivity. The apostle Peter tells us that a woman must be honored "as the weaker partner"; however, he reminds us that the man must also be loved and respected: *"So again I say, each man must love his wife as he loves himself, and the wife must respect her husband."* (Ephesians 5:33)

When a wife respects her husband, she is showing sensitivity to his heart. Women should remember that Biblically, the man is the head of the relationship. As a result, when the wife allows the husband to maintain his position as head of the household, she will show honor and respect, having a lasting and positive effect in his life.

OBSTACLES TO SENSITIVITY

Sensitivity to love is revealed by letting a man know that he rules the household. When this happens, the man will shower his wife with all the love he feels for her. So then, what are some of the obstacles that prevent the manifestation of sensitivity in a relationship? Consider the following:

- ❑ Sensitivity cannot manifest itself under pride.
- ❑ Sensitivity cannot manifest itself under jealousy.
- ❑ Sensitivity cannot manifest itself under fear.
- ❑ Sensitivity cannot manifest itself under infidelity.
- ❑ Sensitivity cannot manifest itself under pressure from the past.

Without a doubt, these are obstacles that will keep a couple from being sensitive to love. One cannot be sensitive to love while at the same time have a root of bitterness or live with resentments carried over from the past. In order to be more sensitive to love, a couple must first cleanse their heart of any injury that was caused by words or actions that expressed the opposite of love in the relationship. One cannot deposit love into a hurting heart, and cannot promise something if there is still mistrust. Furthermore, one cannot show affection, devotion or love without first revealing a repented heart. In short, the couple cannot even begin to imagine that everything is fine if there is un-forgiveness.

WHAT IS LOST IN THE RELATIONSHIP

Many of our counseling sessions in my office have revealed to Raquel and I that there is a lack of sensibility between couples. Along with the loss of sensibility to love within the heart, mutual respect has also been lost. When couples are sensitive, they can feel through physical and moral ways. "Feeling" is like the "touch" of the five senses. In a relationship, the couple must be able to reach the heart of the loved one and "touch" their emotions. Emotions are the manifestation of what one feels in the heart. Feelings are the effects; the action of feeling. If the couple cannot sense each other's feelings, they are not reaching their hearts.

Many relationships are superficial, and their actions are external, rather than internal. They know how to meet external needs, but are unable to reach internal needs. For example, a hug or a kiss are an external need, but when a man can have time alone with his wife in a romantic setting, and express his love with soft and loving words, he will reach the most sensitive part of her heart.

Sexual intercourse is a good example of sensibility to love as an outward expression, where satisfaction is limited to the act itself. Sexual intercourse is a mental desire, not a desire of the heart. Nevertheless, it can be a sensitive, deep and lasting act. Sexual intercourse takes time, and it seeks to fill your spouse's need, not merely your own. Exploration in lovemaking can bring joy that satisfies both partners. This is what it means to be sensible to love. Sensitive love endures everything; it is kind, it is loving, it is patient, it is the main foundation of a relationship. When a couple is attentive and caring toward each other, they will always be sensible to love. Love is expressed in many ways, but most of all, it is seen as it develops into the basis of fulfilled happiness and joy in the marriage.

HOW CAN WE BE SENSITIVE?

We are not all born with sensibility to love. Love is birthed and develops as it is practiced. Feelings are connected to the soul and emotions, which in turn, are connected to the heart. The human being is tripartite with spirit, soul, and body. Every person has feelings, but not all know how to express emotions. Love, for example, is an intense feeling that needs to manifest itself through emotions. As these two elements are connected, sensitivity arises within the heart.

In my own case, I am sensitive to Raquel's needs because I love her deeply, and because I love her with all my heart, my feelings for her are true. It is therefore my responsibility as a husband, to care for her emotional and physical health since we both promised to love each other in adversity, sickness, wealth or poverty, until death do us part. Consider again what the apostle Peter tells us:

In 1 Peter 3:7, Peter is telling husbands to act honorably with their wives, to be sensitive to their needs, and to care for them as one would with fragile glass,[2] because they are not just any common object. There are many great Biblical principles that help strengthen the union between a husband and wife, but the problem is that not everyone is looking for them. Couples are only sensible when they are madly in love with each other.

SENSITIVITY STRENGTHENS UNITY

One of the benefits of being sensible to love is that it strengthens the sense of oneness in the relationship. Sensitivity unites a couple with a seal of security. When I am sensible to Raquel, she feels safe being by my side because she knows that I am aware of her needs. This strengthens her self-confidence, knowing that nothing bad will come to her heart as I will be there to protect her.

Similarly, Raquel is sensitive to my needs and my heart. When we were senior pastors in our church, along with my various other responsibilities, Raquel was very sensitive about how I would feel physically, mentally, emotionally, and spiritually. She was sensitive to the times I needed, rest, when I felt hungry or if I just needed a love hug and tender kisses from her. To this day, Raquel is still able to meet all my needs. Even when she is concerned about my health and well-being, I feel well cared for and loved by her, my best friend and lover.

Set time aside in your daily life to practice being sensitive to the love of your life. Be sensitive to your spouse's needs through kindness and understanding. Show affection, and learn to listen to each other's hearts.

---

[2] A Spanish version of the Bible, the Reina Valera 1960, translates "weaker partner" as "a more fragile glass, or container," from the Greek word σκεῦος (skeuos), meaning "a vessel, utensil for containing anything".

LACK OF SENSITIVITY HARDENS THE HEART

Now we come to a dangerous part in sensibility. When there is a lack of sensibility to love, the heart will invariably become hardened. One who does not protect the heart, or the needs of a spouse, will eventually become the insensible, immature, and irresponsible spouse in the relationship. There are other factors that explain why this type of behavior may occur, including the childhood environment and the manner in which one was raised. It could also be the consequence of the kind of friends with which one associates. There is an old Armenian proverb that says "Tell me who your friends are, and I will tell you who you are."

Some individuals can be persons with a strong character and may find it hard to understand the importance of being sensitive in every aspect. So, when they are not sensitive to love, they begin to establish barriers that reject gentle touching, attention, and even moments alone with the spouse. This type of behavior causes the heart to harden itself to the expressing of emotions and, as in the end, to love itself. Proverbs 14:10 puts it this way: *"Each heart knows its own bitterness, and no one else can fully share its joy."*

On many occasions this type of behavior leads a person to create distance, even to the point of looking for a way out of the relationship. These are unhappy people, confused, and unable to love. Anyone with this type of behavior should seek immediate help.

A WOUNDED HEART IS NOT SENSITIVE

Many of the couples we counsel, arrive to our office with an assortment of problems. However, when we see the whole picture, we realize that there is generally something hidden from the past, usually in some form of unresolved conflict. It is a stage in which they were hurt and were victims of mistreatment, abuse or even rape, which form a barrier and prevents them from being sensitive to love.

A heart with deep wounds becomes infected by pain, rejection, bitterness, resentment, and un-forgiveness. Together, these negative emotions block out the flow of positive feelings and love towards their spouse, causing the emotions to dry up internally and eventually leading to an indifference regarding the needs of the marriage.

Many couples are in a marriage without really having come to know each other well. Once married, however, they realize that the other is not the same person as before. The easiest thing to do, they imagine, is to leave the relationship. Yet, every problem has its solution.

A person like this needs is a Christian counselor to help break down the bonds and learn to forgive those that have hurt them in their past. The key is learning to forgive those who have caused harm with evil actions and words, and seek restoration under the power of the Holy Spirit. Without a doubt, the result will be a healthy marriage and a new heart with which to demonstrate sensitivity to love.

CHAPTER 7

EXPRESS YOUR LOVE IN PUBLIC

"He escorts me to the banquet hall; it's obvious how much he loves me."

SONG OF SOLOMON 2:4

One of the most romantic steps to love that can exist in a relationship, is being able to express love in public. Keep in mind that love is not merely a sexual expression, but a fruit of the spirit. As individuals, we inevitably change over the years, but love is something that should never change. The most beautiful aspect about genuine love is being able to express it freely. Demonstrations of love are not intended to be reserved only for the bedroom, but rather to be expressed in public as well.

Love can be expressed in five different ways; through the five senses of hearing, sight, smell, taste, and touch. I can express love to Raquel by stroking her hair or merely touching her cheeks. I see her beauty from head to toe, and long to hold her in my arms. As I embrace her and smell her perfume, I can sense an intimate desire to be with her. Hearing her soft, tender words only adds to my feelings for her. Love does not always have to be expressed in the same way; it calls for creativity on our part.

BUILDING A WALL OF PROTECTION

When we express our love publicly, we are building a wall of protection. By publicly demonstrating our love for the spouse in our life, we slam the door shut on the enemy. What's more, we are declaring that the person by our side already has a committed spouse, is happy, and there is no access allowed to enter his or her personal area. Whenever we demonstrate our love publicly, we establish the fact that we care and love our relationship well. Aside from protection, it is also a romantic demonstration. If you walk along holding hands, embracing, and kissing each other on the lips in public, you express that a deep and intimate relationship exists.

When Raquel and I go out to eat at a restaurant, we usually observe other couples dining, and can see the differences that couples share at their tables. On one hand, we notice a young couple sitting close together, talking with each other, sharing from the same plate of food and drink, and even feeding bites to each other. Then we observe how older couples sit on opposite sides of the table with limited conversation. They no longer share the same plate of food, they have their own drinks, and don't use the same cutlery. What happened to those special moments when those newlywed couples shared their plates with each other?

Couples demonstrate love in public with words and gestures, and it is not something that is difficult to do when they are truly, in love. Many couples are not overly expressive in public because they believe that love should be something private or something personal that is to be demonstrated only in the privacy of one's home. Others may be embarrassed when it comes to expressing their love in public because they were raised in a very rigid environment. All of these excuses for why love should not be expressed in public can be eliminated. Understand that the expression of love is a manifestation of our feelings. So, we can express our love with words and in a physical manner. For some it may come easily; for others it may be more difficult.

Learn to demonstrate your love in public by using your five senses. Focus on the person you love the most, and forget about the people around you.

LOVE IS THE FOUNDATION

Love is the true foundation of a relationship. There should be no barriers to keep you from expressing love for your spouse. Shame is a result of insecurity and that insecurity, in turn, is a manifestation of weakness. Never let shame weaken the foundation of your relationship.

Why be like past generations that shunned public demonstrations of affection? Why is it necessary to hide behind four walls to express your love? Jesus himself revealed his love for humanity by exposing himself publicly on a cross. So why is there a problem? As parents, you can be living examples of love to your children by showing them that God's love is pure and clean.

For some people it may be somewhat uncomfortable to even hold hands in public, much less embrace. However, for everything there is a beginning and in the case of expressing love, it can be just holding hands while walking. This can be followed by a hug, and at the end of the night, a tender and affectionate kiss. The expression of

67

love in public places, breaks the bondage of past historical hurts and establishes a fresh new relationship that will benefit your children and future generations to come.

If the Lord can reward us in public, according to Matthew 6:4, why is it not possible for a spouse to reward his or her spouse in the same way? We cannot live in silence and fail to express all the love that exists in the unity of a marriage centered on Christ. How is it possible that God's love for a brother or sister can be expressed through Christ in a church, but not be freely expressed with a spouse in public? Ecclesiastes 1:8 says: *"Everything is wearisome beyond description. No matter how much we see, we are never satisfied. No matter how much we hear, we are not content."*

There are many women who prefer that their husbands not touch them in public places or shower them openly with love. They may even get upset by the way their husbands express love to them in public. In a number of our counseling sessions with couples, Raquel and I have seen how one or another in the relationship cannot bear what they see or hear from the spouse. In essence, they just plainly dislike being the recipients of loving expressions or behavior in public.

There should always be certain limitations to public expressions of love and in the same manner, we should not feel inhibited to manifest love openly. When there is no guilt, there is no need to react as Adam and Eve did when they hid from the presence of God upon realizing that they were naked. The expression of love in public is not a sin so there should be no reason to hide that from anyone.

THE FIELD TEST

When a couple expresses their love in public, it reveals several things. First, it shows that there is a high level of security in the relationship. Secondly, confidence is revealed. In many couples one of the two tends to be shyer when it comes to being affectionate in public. For some, this may be the result of having been taught that love is to be demonstrated only in private. This is one of the reasons for sin to overflow in our society, because the real model of love has been hidden for hundreds of years.

So, what kind of example then are we setting for our children? Love is a means for setting and shaping new foundations. The simple act of walking hand in hand through a mall, kissing one's spouse in front of the children, or simply embracing outside a restaurant, can reveal one of the many outward expressions of love.

Outward expressions become demonstrations of your love; the certainty that the person by your side is the one person you want everyone to know that you love deeply. This indicates to others that the person you are with already belongs to someone with strong moral values and who is completely in love with them. Nothing and no one can come between the two of you because your love is demonstrable, evident, and in good taste. Women desire the protection of their husbands and one of the ways that husbands can show their love for them is by expressing their love in public. This not only provides a sense of security, but also the added value of what women desire in a romantic sense.

HOW WE REVEAL OUR TRUE SELVES

When a couple shows signs of their love in public, they are showing their true selves. In essence, they are revealing that they are...

❏ Deeply in love each other.

❏ Unashamed to express their mutual affection in public.
❏ Secure in their love for one another.
❏ Free to express themselves.

Two people in love reveal who and what they are, as well as what they will continue to be. Love is an expression that fills the air with a aromatic perfume that everyone can appreciate and enjoy. For example, whenever Raquel sees a young couple expressing a romantic moment with a strong kiss, she turns to look me in the eye as if asking if I am going to respond in a similar way. This is because showing love for each other in public is infectious and can spread very quickly to others. Exhibit what you are: two married people in love, without any concern for what others may think or say, they are truly demonstrating the fact that they are two people in love.

Public demonstrations of love strengthen the bonds of oneness between married couples through mutual sensitivity and devotion in the deepest sense of harmony. Since God has united two people and transformed them into one flesh, it is perfectly okay for them to demonstrate their love even in public places.

CHAPTER **8**

REMAINING FAITHFUL

> **"But if you remain faithful even when facing death, I will give you the crown of life."**
>
> REVELATION 2:10

Faithfulness is loyalty, and that implies putting into practice the faith that someone has in another person. In other words, it is the fulfilment of a commitment to be firm and constant in one's affections. Marriage is a commitment to maintaining unity and manifesting itself in loving and respectful protection of each other.

In our marriage conferences, the main question people ask is: What is the key to remain pure and faithful in a marriage? In today's world there is so much freedom in marital relationships that the guard is lowered regarding the protection of the unity between a husband and wife. Technology has become one of the major weapons that the enemy has used to infiltrate and destroy the sacred bonds of marriage. For example, the constant sending of text messages through cell phones, as well as Facebook, WhatsApp,

Twitter, Instagram, and many other new internet sources that has caused an explosive revolution of infidelity in marriages.

Thus, we must correctly analyze the question: What is the key to remaining faithful in the marriage? The answer is in this word "remain" that means to continue, endure, persist, last, and to preserve your being. What Raquel and I see in most of our counseling sessions is that married couples today do not remain in their relationship under normal conditions. The relationship is not maintained. When respect between the two has been lost, there is no interest in guarding against potential romantic encounters from outside the marriage, and this can destroy any credibility in the union. They are two married people but live separate lives. They have their own lifestyle, their separate friends, and the freedom to do or undo whatever they desire. In their neglect of each other over time, they have allowed the enemy to gradually enter and bring about the destruction of their marriage covenant.

To illustrate this, we can use Facebook, which is one of the most popular forms of communication today for millions of people worldwide. Some men may have more women as "friends" than men. Likewise, there are women who have more men as "friends" than women. You cannot ignore the possibility of something else taking place in the form of a new intimate friendship, you must guard your own life against any unhealthy opportunity that may come.

HOW TO CARE FOR YOUR MARRIAGE

Communication in the marriage is critically important, and that involves being open and honest with each other. You cannot ignore the possibility that the enemy can use a friend, either male or female, to create destructive tendencies in your life.

Following are three steps you should take in protecting your marriage from any illicit opportunities:

- ❏ **Step One:** Limit friendships with people of the opposite sex unless they are friends as well of your spouse. This avoids the possibility of falling into a temporary relationship and, at the same time, strengthens the trust between the two of you.

- ❏ **Step Two:** A married couple must share private passwords of all entries to computer systems, cell phones, electronic devices, etc. There must never be such privacy in a marriage. Husbands and wives should be transparent with each other without any attempts to hide or cover anything. This will strengthen their mutual commitment and stop the enemy's schemes from entering the relationship.

- ❏ **Step Three:** Never go anywhere alone with someone of the opposite sex. Always protect yourself from any opportunity that could damage your personal reputation or your Christian testimony. Try to have at least one other person present if it is necessary.

Many years ago, I worked for Bank of America headquarters along with some 2,500 employees. My colleagues knew that I was a pastor back then and I held a good reputation as a result of my conduct and good testimony. One day a woman who happened to be the wife of a minister, came to me for advice regarding her marriage.

At first, I saw nothing wrong with spending a few minutes with her in the company cafeteria.

To my surprise, however, she told me that her relationship with her husband was not going well and that she wanted to have a relationship with me. My insides shuddered and my jaw dropped. I did not know what to say to her, because nothing like this had ever happened to me. At that moment, I thought to myself, "Dear Lord, please help me out here!" Quickly I said, "I´m sorry, but I am very happily married with my wife and I would not exchange her for anything or anyone else in the world. I said to her that she needed to talk to her pastor and explain to him that she is having problems in her marriage.

Returning immediately to my desk, I called Raquel to tell her what had just happened. I knew that this attack could have come only from the enemy. At first, Raquel felt somewhat uneasy, but quickly realized that in my being honest with her, there was no need at all to feel badly. God brought a supernatural peace between us that strengthened our relationship in that moment.

One month later, I received a call at my office from Raquel. She said, "David, you are *not* going to believe what just happened to me. A man from another department came to my office to tell me that he wants to have a relationship with me and asked if there was any possibility that we could be together for the weekend." It was my turn to feel uncomfortable, but then the Lord reminded me of my own situation just one month previously. That night we were both able to appreciate how important mutual honesty and openness was for the growth of our marriage relationship.

Raquel and I have been able to overcome many obstacles in our married life. And though it has not been easy all these years, we have been able to recognize the importance of being open and honest in everything we live to do. This brings me to a very important step in how to remain faithful in a relationship. More than sincerity, we must be willing to accept mistakes and weaknesses from our spouse. We must know how to establish trust while being sensible to the person we love, knowing and understanding their heart, and filling it with the certainty that there is no other person in our life. It is not enough to just say the words "I love you"; it must also be lived out, learning to demonstrate love through our tender acts of care. We must also learn how to sow the seeds of love in both of our lives in order to reap the good fruit. If we don't sow into our spouse's life, we cannot expect a great harvest.

Faithfulness must be mutual between a married couple and not just one-sided. Unfaithfulness, on the other hand, is not only being unfaithful to your spouse with another person, but it can also mean being unfaithful in many other aspects, such as work, finances, addictions, relationships with one's in-laws, and even with children in the marriage. Your married life should be made a priority above anything else. Never allow others to steal your time together as a marriage and as a family. As a result, you will in turn, be able to enjoy time with God as well as with each other.

BE FAITHFUL

In the Bible we find an exhortation that we must always keep in mind: *"Be on guard. Stand firm in the faith. Be courageous. Be strong. And do everything with love."* (1 Corinthians 16:13-14)

When one person says to another "be faithful" a typical response could be "faithful to what?" First and foremost, we need to be faithful to God. Every time our faithfulness to God begins to slacken, we may find that our faithfulness to our spouse is also beginning to falter. The key to a marriage remaining "until death do us part" is in being faithful to your spouse. Just as faithfulness is a pillar in the life of a believer, so faithfulness must be a pillar in married life.

Faithfulness builds and sustains the life of a healthy married relationship. Fidelity is like a thread of life that continues to believe in bringing about healing and reconciliation when a relationship has gone through rough times. Because faithfulness is so important in a relationship, it hurts deeply when it disappears from a marriage. When one of the two is unfaithful, the resulting pain goes beyond any other type of pain. Betrayal hurts deeply and inevitably leads to anger and disappointment.

The only Biblical reason given by Jesus for the dissolution of a marriage is unfaithfulness; in other words, the lack of faithfulness through adultery, leads to a total loss of trust in the marriage. Since faithfulness is at the core of marriage, when there is no faithfulness in the relationship, other aspects of the marriage cannot function according to God's plan. How can one remain committed to a person who has been unfaithful? How can one communicate on a deeper level if the other person is creating a breach of trust that has turned into an unattainable situation?

Without God's help a healthy marriage is difficult to maintain. So why is faithfulness so important to God? Because when we decide of our own free will to be faithful to God, he gives us the ability to be faithful to each other. The desire to be faithful no longer rests solely on one person because the relationship is centered on God's will. The power of the Holy Spirit helps us to stay faithful, not only in our daily walk with the Lord, but also in our walk with our spouse. When we remove God from our life, we lose all the privileges we have in him. Regarding this, the Bible encourages us by making sure we understand that God is always faithful:

"The temptations in your life are no different from what others experience. And God is faithful. He will not allow the temptation to be more than you can stand. When you are tempted, he will show you a way out so that you can endure."

(1 CORINTHIANS 10:13)

WHAT IS FAITHFULNESS?

Faithful people are those who are constant in their affections, in the fulfillment of their obligations, and do not disappoint the trust placed on them. Hence, faithful people are firm and determined. The word "determined" means wanting to do something very much and not allowing anyone or any difficulties to deter you. Faithfulness, then is demonstrated when we are determined in our loyalty, in our affections, and in our creativity to demonstrate these affections.

❏ **Determine to be loyal:** To be faithful is to be loyal. So, when we stand firm with the person we love, we will be faithful to him or her, no matter what. If we are faithful to our spouse, we will be fervent, sincere and true, making an extra effort to hold true to our vows. When we are faithful, we choose to strictly follow the promise we made to our partner before getting married, as well as the vows and promises made on the wedding day. This is a standard by which we should live daily.

❏ **Determine to show affection:** Loyalty also means that we are firm and unchanging in showing our affections in our marriage. This also implies that an affectionate person is patient. For example, if we are not patient and overlook the need for romanticism, we may not have a good, intimate, and satisfying relationship. The affectionate person is also persistent. For this reason, when one does not feel a genuine interest in being affectionate in the marital bed, look for the reason, change the conditions and tomorrow everything will be different.

❏ **Determine to be creative:** Faithfulness in our affections requires that we use our creative imagination. If what we've done in the past to arouse each other doesn't work today, try something new. There should never be any limits to what can be done in the bedroom. Step away from the routine and look for new ways to enjoy and satisfy each other. When advice is needed in this area, seek the guidance of a Christian counselor.

PATTERNS OF INFIDELITY

There are various patterns of behavior that are evident in a marriage where there has been unfaithfulness from either part. First, unfaithfulness develops in the mind and is linked to sexual immorality that leads the person to look outside of the marriage for a temporary satisfaction of sexual desires. Secondly, infidelity occurs in those who seek to leave the marriage because their relationship is drying up and they have grown distant from each other. Whatever the reason, this unfaithfulness is adultery before God: *"You have heard the commandment that says, 'You must not commit adultery.' But I say, anyone who even looks at a woman with lust has already committed adultery with her in his heart.*" (Matthew 5:27-28)

In this Bible text, Jesus is very clear regarding adultery. He even goes so far as to say that even if we look at a woman (or a man) with lust, we have already committed adultery in our heart. When we give ourselves completely, there should be no desire to be with someone else. According to Galatians 5:19, 21, neither the adulterer nor the fornicator will inherit the kingdom of God: *"When you follow the desires of your sinful nature, the results are very clear: sexual immorality, impurity, lustful pleasures... Let me tell you again, as I have before, that anyone living that sort of life will not inherit the Kingdom of God."*

Here's a look at some of the behavioral patterns revealed by people who are unfaithful:

- ❏ Showing a lack of interest in sexual intercourse.
- ❏ Giving excuses for going out late at night.
- ❏ Arriving late from work.
- ❏ Going aside to talk on the phone.
- ❏ Taking a shower after returning from an appointment.
- ❏ Refusing to give passwords to each other of a cell phone or computer.
- ❏ Not wanting a joint bank account.
- ❏ Constantly being in a foul mood.
- ❏ Changing personal appearance and style of clothes.
- ❏ Taking long trips on "work" related issues.

All of these patterns can be signs of unfaithfulness and possible involvement with someone else that will ultimately destroy the marriage. In such cases, it is best to seek professional help on how to deal with the consequences of sin and restore the marriage. In many cases, a pastor cannot always help in these situations because they may not be equipped or prepared to help with counseling at this level of the marital problem.

THE CONSEQUENCES OF UNFAITHFULNESS

In most cases of infidelity, the consequences are destructive and they ultimately end in divorce. There is nothing worse than seeing a marriage destroyed, and the family torn apart as a result of unfaithfulness. When a husband and wife's relationship has been divided, the consequences are always severe, not only for the married couple, but also for the children. Everything that the two have built together as a married couple is lost. The respect and dignity of the marriage is lost along with all the good memories and dreams they built together.

Unfaithfulness leaves a lasting scar in the heart of the one who has been deceived, marking his or her life with pain, contempt, and perhaps feelings of revenge. Once a person has been unfaithful to their spouse, he or she will likely be unfaithful to others because this is a bondage of the soul that only God can heal and liberate.

God's Word says: *"Give honor to marriage, and remain faithful to one another in marriage. God will surely judge people who are immoral and those who commit adultery."* (Hebrews 13:4) Furthermore, the result of the sin of unfaithfulness is death: *"For the wages of sin is death..."* (Romans 6:23). The end result is death to one's spirit, to one's dreams, to one's future, including the previous relationship with one's spouse.

THE RESTORATION OF UNFAITHFULNESS

It is not easy to restore a marriage that has suffered infidelity or adultery. There are consequences to sin, and one must realize the destruction that has come into the home. So then, what happens after this kind of tragedy? What happens after the storm? Is restoration even possible?

According to the Scriptures, adultery is the only reason God accepts one to issue a certificate of divorce:

❏ "You have heard the law that says, 'A man can divorce his wife by merely giving her a written notice of divorce." (Matthew 5:31)

❏ "Whoever divorces his wife and marries someone else commits adultery against her. And if a woman divorces her husband and marries someone else, she commits adultery." (Mark 10:11-12)

In other words, the one who leaves the home for another relationship provides the spouse the right to give him a certificate of divorce. This does not mean that one is not under an obligation to divorce out of obligation, but only that one has the legal right to do so.

The ideal situation would be to attempt to restitute and restore the relationship, bringing about restitution through the grace of God. This kind of restoration can best be done with the help and guidance of a good Christian counselor. The married couple must go through extensive counseling sessions in order to heal and restore the marriage. Furthermore, the one who committed adultery must be counseled in a deeper level to be liberated from any bondage in the soul to break any legal rights that has been given to the enemy.

CHAPTER 9

INVEST TIME IN EACH OTHER

"For everything there is a season, a time for every activity under heaven."

ECCLESIASTES 3:1

L ife itself is full of the investments that we make. We invest our money in the stock market, our energy at the gym, and our time in sports. What's more, we invest in homes, cars, clothes, cell phones, large-screen televisions, shopping, manicures and pedicures, etc. We invest in thousands of different things in life, but rarely do we invest in the life of our spouse. Is it so difficult to invest in the life of the person who we love the most? It's quite amazing to hear the complaints in my office from couples who are tired of living with their spouse simply because they are unwilling to invest the time it takes to strengthen the marriage.

It is important to understand that in order to invest in something, there must be a compelling interest. In the same way that we invest money in the bank and earn interest each month, we should also learn to invest in the relationship with our spouse. The key, however, is in the size of the deposit that we make. The more we deposit genuine love into the relationship, the greater the return will be.

Raquel is very creative and fanatical in finding time for us to have fun together. Not a single day goes by without her wanting to go for a walk together or go to the gym, take a bike ride, go to the beach, stroll through a mall or just sit down at home to watch a romantic movie. (I must confess that I try to get her to watch an action movie from time to time!) With all that and more, at the heart of what she really wants is that we take TIME to be together. This is why spending time with one's spouse is so important.

We lead very busy lives. If I am not in a meeting with other pastors, I am in zoom meetings with ministry colleagues of other nations. We participate in regular church activities, and also accept speaking engagements to other churches throughout the nation. We are guest speakers for many marriage conferences, and at times, it is an honor for me to attend meetings with city and government officials in the various countries that we visit and minister. At the end of the day, there is little time remaining for my personal life. Yet, I have learned to invest good quality time with Raquel because I value the moments we get to spend together. She takes priority over ministry, meetings, and scheduled events.

HOW TO MANAGE TIME

A problem that Raquel and I have seen in many couples is that they do not know how to manage or prioritize their time. Their lives are disordered. When they try to find time to spend together, it rarely seems to be available. Couples need to learn how to manage and prioritize both family time and time for the marriage itself, because everything has its order and place.

The following steps are the order in which God would have us prioritize our time:

1. **God:** Putting God first is the most important part of our spiritual life because he is the one who gives direction and instruction for everything we do in life. Without God we cannot be a good husband or wife.

2. **Marriage:** One's spouse is the next integral part of life. When a couple has sworn their undying love for each other in their wedding vows, they have established a covenant between themselves and with God, that they would live together according to what he has ordained for holy matrimony. They promised to love, honor, respect, help, and care for one another in times of sickness and health, in prosperity and in adversity, remaining faithful until separated by death. Nothing in life should ever replace that covenant.

3. **Family:** If the couple has children, these would be the next in God's order. Children do not take priority over the marriage since they did not come first. Children grow up and leave the home, but the marriage continues. The marriage came before there were children.

4. **Work:** Work is very important in the family, but it is not the foundation. Many believe that without money the family unit will not function. Love is significantly more valuable than money itself. Love is the ingredient that unites the

family, strengthens the home, and nurtures the marriage. Employment may change from one day to the next, but a Christ-centered family will remain forever.

5. **Ministry:** The church is a major part of the family and helps to provide unity and maintain spiritual stability in everyday life. A church or ministry should not be a substitute for family time, and a good balance should be maintained between church and family. If there are three or more days of participation in church activities and there is only one day for the family to spend together, that shows that there is an imbalance.

This then is God's order for a healthy home: When a couple establishes and maintains the order listed above, then God is glorified when we find the proper time to invest and build a strong healthy family. There should be no excuse for a married couple to not know how to invest time with each other.

THE INVESTMENT OF TIME

Following are some important guidelines for a couple to learn how to spend time with each other:

❏ Set aside at least one day a week for the two of you. On those days, spend several hours together without the children. Discover activities that are out of the routine that both of you can enjoy.

❑ Once every two or four weeks, depending on the budget, go out for a romantic dinner, just the two of you. On these nights, do not invite other couples, or take the children.

❑ Once every three months, also depending on the budget, spend a romantic night in a nice hotel. Take time to talk with each other, especially expressing your love for one another.

❑ Invest in an annual vacation. Every married couple as a family, should take time out for rest and relaxation after a year of hard work. This type of activity helps to strengthen the relationship between a husband and wife as well as with the children.

Following these guidelines regularly will benefit the marriage in the long run. There is nothing more important than strengthening the unity between a husband and wife, and the best way to do this is with good invested time together.

WHEN WE LOSE TRACK OF TIME

Time is of the essence. Without any doubt, time is an ingredient of great importance in a marriage. Life is surrounded by time, the special moments, and hours of investment. There should never be a dull moment when we are happy and content with the person that we love.

Raquel and I have been married for over forty years and we feel that the weeks, months, and years have gone by all too fast. Our children are grown adults, each with their own lives, and have given us the blessing of grandchildren. We have traveled all over the world, and we've had the honor of pastoring an amazing congregation for twenty-seven years, that have loved and respected us greatly. My question is: "How is it possible that time in our lives has flown by so fast? It seems like just yesterday that our children were babies!" When you see how time flies, keep the following in mind:

- ❑ Do not waste your time with friends if your spouse is your best friend.
- ❑ Do not waste your time with overtime at your job if your family needs you at home.
- ❑ Do not waste your time with your hobbies and neglect your marriage.
- ❑ Do not waste your time, rather learn to invest time in each other.

When we think about it, we suddenly realize how impossible it is to make up for lost time: *"History merely repeats itself. It has all been done before. Nothing under the sun is truly new."* (Ecclesiastes 1:9)

TIME THAT IS NEEDED

How much time does it take to have a healthy marriage? How much time should be invested in a relationship to keep it happy? The Bible tells us that time is very valuable in life: "For everything there is a season, a time for every activity under heaven." (Ecclesiastes 3:1)

Always remember that it is not necessarily about the quantity of time, but the quality of the time that you spend together. "There is a time for everything," says the Preacher in Ecclesiastes, but the quality of time is what restores and strengthens relationships. How long does it take to build a five-story building? It all depends on the investment, the quality of the materials, and the size of the structure. The best always requires more time and attention, but whatever is done fast and with cheap materials, will eventually bring destruction. The same is true in your relationship; slow down and invest your time with the person that you love and enjoy:

- ❑ Prepare your relationship well.
- ❑ Have a plan.
- ❑ Establish a good foundation.
- ❑ Enjoy each other in the present.

Time comes and goes, but when you plan your future well, life will never be boring!

TIME NEVER ENDS

We often hear the expressions "My time is up" or "I don't have any more time." These same individuals should ask themselves: "How is it possible that I am out of time when the clock is still ticking?" or "How can it be that there is no time to do what I have to do?"

Time is a never-ending element that extends through your entire lifetime. Time has no expiration date, so determine to live each day to the fullest. There are no guarantees regarding tomorrow for anyone. The Bible says: *"Make the most of every opportunity in these evil days."* (Ephesians 5:16)

You really have no idea what tomorrow may bring, not even knowing whether you will be alive or dead. A good practice is to live each day as if it were your last day on earth, enjoying it to the fullest with the person that you love. While time has no end, every person will eventually run out of time on earth. So enjoy life, enjoy each moment, enjoy each hour, and rejoice in the joy of marriage by spending time together, I assure you that life will have much more meaning with each passing day!

CHAPTER 10

THE IMPORTANCE OF BEING ONE IN MARRIAGE

> **"That is why a man leaves his father and mother and is united to his wife, and they become one flesh."**
>
> **GENESIS 2:24 (NIV)**

It is no coincidence that the very first marital union in human history is presented at the very beginning of the Scriptures. In the book of Genesis, the word "unite" in the original language of the Old Testament, has a very profound meaning. The translation from Hebrew is "to adhere, to hold, to join fast together, to cling, to join, to strengthen".[3] It implies two people who have come together face to face, skin to skin, and become one flesh.

It is rather unique that in all of God's creation, only humans are sexually intimate in a face-to-face manner. It is important to understand that "uniting" is more than just a sexual reference. The

---

[3] Strong's Hebrew Lexicon.

word "unite" implies a spiritual and emotional union. This verse in Genesis makes silence for men. Most women feel loved when their husbands express their love in ways that are not sexual in nature. As for "touching" we all know that physical touch is one way of communicating love in an emotional way.

There has been much research in the field of child development with regard to the newborn, and one of the great discoveries has to do with physical touch. Infants that are held, carried, hugged, and kissed, develop a much healthier emotional life than those who are left alone for long periods of time with no physical contact.

The same is true in a marriage. Physical touch is a powerful means of communicating love in a marriage. The simple act of holding hands, kissing throughout the day, hugging often, and even sexual intimacy are ways of communicating that emotional love. For most women, physical touch becomes a primary form of love. Wives feel safe when their husbands touch and hold them.

In Deuteronomy 24:5 we see what closeness in marriage means: *"A newly married man must not be drafted into the army or be given any other official responsibilities. He must be free to spend one year at home, bringing happiness to the wife he has married."*

Can you imagine what this man would do to make his wife happy? This fascinating passage demonstrates how well God's people in the past, understood the values that are important in a marriage. They knew that the first year of marriage was essential in establishing a foundation of oneness in the relationship before entering the battlefield, before the demands of providing for the family, before other problems could arise.

Today's world is quite different than it was thousands of years ago for the people of Israel. In a contemporary marriage, it would not be realistic for a couple to spend their first years together without ever being apart from each other. What is possible, however, is to establish a positive atmosphere every day after returning home from work. After being apart all day, the first few minutes are crucial in order to reconnect with each other, setting the mood for the rest of the day.

What makes matter worse in our current society today, are the economic pressures demanding that both spouses work. This can easily create a distancing, or separation, due to weariness and fatigue. Spouses must touch each other as often as possible. A husband may return home later than his wife, but the basic dynamics of the unit still fit any situation. There is no excuse for not kissing your wife when you arrive home, touching her, or telling her that you missed her all day and that she means everything to you. Men need to know that women long for connection.

WHEN A WOMAN FEELS CLOSE

The following list presents things that a man can do to make a woman feel close to her husband. A woman experiences closeness to her husband when he:

- ❑ Holds her hand.
- ❑ Hugs her.
- ❑ Is affectionate or loving without sexual intimacy.
- ❑ Takes time to be alone with her and focuses on her and the conversation.
- ❑ Takes her for a walk.
- ❑ Helps to keep the house clean.
- ❑ Takes her out to dinner, without the children.
- ❑ Compliments her and compliments her appearance.
- ❑ Is willing and able to talk to her after making love.

Every man should understand that being close to his wife costs nothing other than time and love. There are even times when perhaps giving her a gift would help seal certain moments together. This however, also depends on the budget.

WHEN A MAN FEELS CLOSE

Since men are very different from women, they have different needs. However, there are things that a wife can do to make her husband feel close to her. A man experiences closeness to his wife when she:

- ❏ Sits on his lap and whispers in his ear.
- ❏ Undresses in his presence.
- ❏ Goes to bed without pajamas.
- ❏ Accompanies him to watch a game.
- ❏ Watches an action movie with him.
- ❏ Allows him to spend time with his friends.

Just as with a man, every woman should know that being close to her husband costs nothing other than time and love. If we look closely at the needs of men and women, they are quite different in many respects. Yet, both are looking for the same thing, only gift-wrapped differently. The problem occurs when neither communicates their needs. So, when a man doesn't know what a woman likes, and she doesn't know what he likes, both assume that the partner knows what he or she likes. Unfortunately, by the time they realize this situation, they have already begun to argue since neither has been able to fill the other's void.

Love is much like a seed that needs sunlight and water to grow. First, love is planted in the life of the other person, then it must be watered with loving words. And lastly, love is nurtured as the rays of encouragement sink in, providing the warmth of appreciation and support. To bring about fruit, however, it is not enough to do just one of these three things. If a couple invests in giving continuously to these three aspects of the relationship, they will enjoy the resulting fruit for the rest of their lives.

The Bible tells us: *"In the same way, husbands ought to love their wives as they love their own bodies. For a man who loves his wife actually shows love for himself."* (Ephesians 5:28) In other words, if every husband loves and gives himself to his wife in this way, such a man would love himself and in return, he will have a happy and loving woman in his life. If a husband demonstrates and practices these principles, he will receive his wife's respect.

UNITY IS A THREE-STRAND CORD

What God has joined cannot be separated, but we cannot ignore the fact that the enemy seeks to destroy marriages that are founded on the solid rock that is Christ Jesus. However, when God is kept at the center of a relationship, the possibility of the enemy hindering and contaminating what the Lord has joined together, may become eliminated. In a Christ-centered marriage Jesus must reign supremely in the relationship and he becomes the third strand of a cord in the relationship, a strand which cannot be broken: *"... a triple-braided cord is not easily broken"* (Ecclesiastes 4:12).

Unity becomes the attribute or quality of what constitutes a whole, comprised of its correlated parts. I am talking about two individuals who constitute a total part, and in turn, forming a single identity. Raquel and I are two separate individuals, but together we form one identity. What is it that unites us? We are united by our love, our commitment, and most of all, by our Lord Jesus Christ.

A marriage will not work effectively if the couple is separated or divided in any respect. Unfortunately, it is not uncommon to see marriages divided in these areas:

- ❏ Separate bank accounts.
- ❏ Separate beds or bedrooms.
- ❏ Separate vacations.
- ❏ In-laws attempting to control the couple.

These are just a few examples of divisions that will eventually destroy the unity of a marriage. Effective unity in a marriage is what Christ demonstrates to us in his Word. Unity strengthens the core foundation of a marriage.

WEAKNESS DESTROYS

The enemy looks to destroy those who are weak. People that are in poor spiritual health are those that are weak. They live with insecurity, lies, and all that is wrong in their own lives including improper and sinful behaviors.

When a couple comes to us for counseling, we are able to identify their weaknesses within the first few minutes. It is not uncommon to see how easily weakness can destroy a once healthy marriage. Weakness can eat a person from the inside. It can also lead to defeat and cause embarrassment in front of others. As a result, weakness makes a person want to give up, robbing one's peace and personal security that is so necessary. The person that is not connected to the Word of God will eventually be defeated, but with God being a strong part of their life, that person will live in victory.

The apostle Paul understood this when he wrote the following: *"My grace is all you need. My power works best in weakness"* (2

Corinthians 12:9). He also wrote that the Lord tells us that when we are weak, he is strong. In fact, he sent the Holy Spirit to help us in our weakness (see Romans 8:26).

We must understand that if we live in a marriage without God's help, our life will eventually be destroyed. So, don't give way to weaknesses that come from all that is negative, keep the heavy load of destruction from falling on your marriage by putting God first in every situation.

STRENGTH BUILDS

In Deuteronomy 6:5, the Bible presents the following command: *"you must love the LORD your God with all your heart, all your soul, and all your strength."*

Here we see three areas by which we should love God: "heart," "soul" and "strength." These areas of strength become the power, the magnitude, and the structure of love. A weakened love does not go very far, as the circumstances of life will devour it, and the lies of this world will destroy it by fire.

The Bible tells us that love *"always protects, always trusts, always hopes, always perseveres"* (1 Corinthians 13:7, NIV). How could love protect from suffering without strength? Without strength, it would be impossible to even attempt to fight, to win, or to conquer. Strength is the motor of a relationship, so to speak, and without it we would not get anywhere.

Strength builds, strength opens a way, strength conquers all, strength never gives up. Strength will help us achieve our dreams and overcome our struggles. Remember that God is the one who can give us strength and remove any obstacle from our path: *"It is God who arms me with strength and keeps my way secure."* (2 Samuel 22:33, NIV)

CHAPTER 11

STRENGTHEN YOUR FRIENDSHIP

"Submit to God, and you will have peace;
then things will go well for you."

JOB 22:21

My best friend is Raquel, and I am certain that she would say the same is true of me. Not only that, but we are also friends "in the Lord" because in our marriage friendship goes hand in hand with our faith. I believe with confidence, that a genuine relationship and a firm foundation of faith are at the heart of every healthy marriage.

Many couples enter marriage thinking that the primary basis for a good marriage is sexual compatibility. Their thinking is; the better the sexual relationship, the better the marriage will be. The more passionate and frequent in sexual intercourse, the stronger the marriage will be. Let me assure you that if you and your spouse do not develop a friendship in the marriage, the sexual relationship

99

will eventually come to a halt. There is a sense of oneness in mutual affection and esteem that is vital to maintaining a healthy sexual relationship. Intimacy becomes an expression of affection and stimulates what is already felt. A good sexual relationship may or may not generate affection and esteem. There are many who merely see each other as a means for sexual gratification, yet in the end, the mutual esteem is diminished.

Through our years of counseling, Raquel and I have met individuals who are not really in love with their spouse with whom they are having a sexual relationship. They only see their spouse as a way to satisfy their own physical needs and sexual desires. It is very common for us to see couples who have not developed a friendship within each other. They have become disconnected, cold, distant, bitter, and unhappy. The way they treat each other is not good-natured, and they speak to each other with sarcastic and hurtful words.

CHARACTERISTICS OF A TRUE FRIEND

It is important to develop a good friendship between a husband and wife, and there are good characteristics that generally show that kind of friendship. Listed below is a list of several characteristics that can **help** you build a good relationship with your spouse:

Friends...
- ❏ Take time to be together.
- ❏ Do things together.
- ❏ Laugh together.
- ❏ Cry together.

- ❏ Have great conversations.
- ❏ Don't keep secrets from each other.
- ❏ Help each other.
- ❏ Trust each other.
- ❏ Are open and honest with each other.

A true friend is one who is close to another person through affection and esteem. A true friend is a pleasant companion who is never hostile, does not abuse, curse or wish harm for the other. A true friend always stands by his friend, and is in full support of that friendship. In the long run, competition is not something that belongs in that true friendship.

A couple that strongly opposes each other will not last long in a relationship. They may not abandon the home physically, but they will disconnect emotionally, placing distance between themselves and their spouse. There may be such a personality change that they become quiet, withdrawn or even depressed. This may lead to one spending more time at work or with other friends, staying away from the family as much as possible, and eventually even becoming involved with another person. This can happen to men and women.

For the most part, wives who dissociate from their husbands choose to spend more time with their mother, their children or their friends than with the husband. They may even choose to withdraw from any sexual act altogether.

In a healthy marriage there should never be any kind of competition. When marriages start to compete, they end up not sharing. Competition can turn out to be a marriage killer when it is about each one looking for applause, recognition, gifts, and even fame. Spouses who have a competitive spirit with each other are very seldom satisfied. These types of individuals will always feel rejected, abandoned, and unappreciated. On top of that, they can become bitter, frustrated, angry, and dissatisfied with life in general. The Bible strongly condemns these attitudes when it speaks of the importance of unity and love among believers in Jesus Christ:

❏ *"Get rid of all bitterness, rage, anger, harsh words, and slander, as well as all types of evil behavior. Instead, be kind to each other, tenderhearted, forgiving one another, just as God through Christ has forgiven you."* (Ephesians 4:31-32)

❏ *"Since God chose you to be the holy people he loves, you must clothe yourselves with tenderhearted mercy, kindness, humility, gentleness, and patience. Make allowance for each other's faults, and forgive anyone who offends you. Remember, the Lord forgave you, so you must forgive others. Above all, clothe yourselves with love, which binds us all together in perfect harmony. And let the peace that comes from Christ rule in your hearts. For as members of one body, you are called to live in peace. And always be thankful."* (Colossians 3:12-15)

The Bible is very straightforward as well when it speaks about marriage, family, and reconciliation: *"There is no longer Jew or Gentile, slave or free, male and female. For you are all one in Christ Jesus."* (Galatians 3:28)

Without love, a marriage is dry and unhappy. Your spouse should be your best friend and that means learning to have great conversations with your spouse about your deepest desires, your greatest fears, and your highest goals in life. Someday your children will leave home, but you will still be married; so, build a friendship that lasts forever.

TRUST

Trust is a manifestation that is developed or established through actions and feelings. The word "trust" implies a "firm hope that you have for someone or something." It also refers to the confidence that one has in oneself.

In marriage there should be trust in the fact that both partners love and respect each other. When trust is broken, however, it is difficult to rebuild a sense of security and hope that the relationship will return to what it once was. Trust is the key to the heart, and once that trust is broken, it is difficult to re-enter a wounded heart: *"Having hope will give you courage. You will be protected and will rest in safety."* (Job 11:18)

One of the most important elements for maintaining a healthy marriage is trust. Trust is a guarantee, an insurance that nothing will come between the two of you. Once trust is lost in a marriage due to infidelity, deceit or dishonesty, it will take time to rebuild because trust is not something you build overnight. Trust develops with much time and investment.

Investment of ...
- ❏ Time
- ❏ Change
- ❏ Sacrifice
- ❏ Sincerity
- ❏ Honesty

Understand that once trust is lost and the marriage is in the process of rebuilding, it may never be the same again. And why? Because now one must live with the consequences, the stain of the past, and the couple will remember the negative impact that has been done.

RESPECT

One of the elements that is very often lost in a relationship is respect. The idea of respect involves the "consideration, esteem, regard, admiration" given to someone. In a healthy relationship, you must respect the other person's feelings and values. The Scriptures are very clear when Paul writes: *"Each man must love his wife as he loves himself, and the wife must respect her husband."* (Ephesians 5:33)

There is a recognition of authority in the person who knows how to respect. Paul indicates something very clear to us in this verse by telling a man that he must "love his wife as he loves himself". With this, we are given to understand that when a man loves his wife as himself, he honors her as part of his very own being. What's more, when a man can show his wife that he loves her, she will respond with respect for him as the head of the household. Keep in mind that respect is earned, it's not something with which one is born. Without respect, the marital connection is broken and the unity between a husband and wife is lost. However, when a man submits to God's authority, he can easily love his wife, and in turn, his wife is able to respect and honor her husband.

SUPPORT

Support is the foundation that allows something to remain strong. In a healthy relationship each must support the other from all points of view. Without support, a relationship has no foundation. As a married couple, the two make a home, so they must learn to support each other to unite in the bond of marriage. A husband needs the support of his wife in order to be efficient in his role as a husband. Similarly, a wife needs her husband's support in order to be efficient in her role as a wife. The support must be mutual, since they both must share the responsibility of the home to make everything work well and stay in unity.

When support is present in a marriage, a couple can rely on each other without any blame. They are no longer two but one flesh, so they put pride aside and work together as a husband and wife. As a husband, I cannot be efficient in my own life without the support of my wife. Likewise, my wife cannot be efficient in her own life without my support.

ACCOUNTABILITY

In a healthy marriage there must be accountability, a type of order to properly account for one's actions. In other words, accountability in a relationship shows up in the way each spouse responds on matters such as:

- ❏ Loyalty
- ❏ Faithfulness
- ❏ Stability
- ❏ Love
- ❏ Respect

In fact, one could add the vows that the two made to each other on their wedding day. Each spouse has to answer with regard to how they keep what was promised, thereby protecting the oneness in their marriage. Without accountability in a marriage, there will be no interest or responsibility in the relationship. What's more, there will never be respect or trust in the relationship. Accountability reminds one of what is good and ensures that nothing will hinder either from keeping their promise, until death shall separate them.

CHAPTER 12

A LIFE-LONG LOVE

"Love will last forever."

1 CORINTHIANS 13:8

I t's so amazing to know that love is for a lifetime! The sad part is that not everyone thinks that way. Love is not just an intense feeling, but also a show of affection, inclination, and total commitment of oneself to the another. Love should last forever. Love should never end. The Bible tells us: *"Love will last forever"* (1 Corinthians 13:8).

The question then is, why do married couples stop loving each other? One of the reasons is that that they perhaps never loved each other. In the process of living together, they come to realize that there never was love, but merely a physical attraction. In other cases, they were unaware of the meaning of love, having entered the bonds of marriage without any premarital counseling.

TO LOVE AND TO BE IN LOVE

Love is the glue that keeps a relationship together. Without love, a relationship cannot not work. It must be understood that love must exist in a marriage if it is to last forever. In marriage, there are two important factors: Love and being in love. "Love" is an action, so when I tell Raquel that I love her, I am expressing a feeling. Feelings, however, can change. "Being in love" on the other hand, is a permanent status. When I declare that I am in love with Raquel, I mean it from deep within my heart, and it is not just a passing feeling.

There are married couples who love each other, but are not necessarily in love. This is one of the reasons why marriages do not last. "To love for a lifetime" is a process. One must learn how to love, not just by expressing their feelings, but rather by what is in their heart. The one who is in love is willing to pay the price, while the one who only loves, but is not *in love*, seeks the benefits without having to pay the price.

I can still remember vividly the night before I married Raquel, when my friends and I went to serenade her. As I mentioned in chapter 4, a favorite song of ours throughout our many years of marriage has been "An Entire Lifetime". The words of this song, performed by the well-known Mexican trio, Los Panchos, and others, reflect perfectly the love I have for Raquel. To be in love for a lifetime, one needs to invest in the life of the loved one. This means spending time alone together, sharing special moments, having loving conversations, and creating unforgettable moments through intimacy.

Love is more than just words; it must also be demonstrated with actions. The couple that does not show this kind of affection, runs the risk of drying the well of love. When this happens, the married couple become roommates and nothing more. When a spouse invests and deposits time, affection, understanding, tenderness, respect, honor, and love into their spouse, there is no doubt that great results will occur. On the other hand, if one does not invest anything at all into the marriage, it is very likely that the relationship will end in dryness and every dream they ever shared will die.

Marriage is formed between two people who are deeply in love. I live to give Raquel all the love she needs to make her feel completely fulfilled in our relationship. In the same way, she lives to give me all the love I need to be joyful and at peace. Happiness is born through true love, and when we come to the full knowledge of loving each other for a lifetime, we understand that there is no reason to seek love elsewhere.

Life itself, is full of complications, differences, problems, anguish, and pain. No matter where you live or how you live, there will always be obstacles. As a married person, you live with the one who will fight alongside you for the rest of your life. You don't have to struggle alone when someone else is by your side to help you grow and build a strong marriage.

One of the things that a woman looks for in a man is security. By this I do not mean merely financial security, but the emotional security found in the heart that enables her to know that her husband will never abandon her in the course of a lifetime. Emotions and feelings have a great influence in women, while men tend to be more logical thinkers. Men can be somewhat crude when it comes to expressing love, while women are more sensitive in expressing their feelings and love for the men in their lives.

THE PROCESS OF LOVING

To love for a lifetime, a couple must go through a long process of living together, yet enjoying the diversity throughout the journey. Each one determines the condition of their life's path, as each steers the wheel and controls the direction. As such, we choose the course, the speed, and the path. When we are in love with our spouse, we must recognize that love should be lasting, eternal, and very memorable. Consequently, in the long process of life we must learn to be creative in how we love our spouse, with whom we will live for the rest of our life. Love expresses itself in several ways:

❏ Through words
❏ Through actions
❏ Through feelings

Learn to develop love for your spouse by incorporating these three factors. They will help to create a solid foundation that will strengthen the marriage relationship. Do not limit your love to just words, actions or feelings. A lifetime of love is expressed using these three factors in combination with each other at all times. It's like saying that love is comprised of several elements. Love is not only a word, but also an action, an expression that carries certain ingredients that demonstrate the intensity of the expression. In order to love someone deeply, it involves a process that takes time. The experience of love makes an amazing journey possible for a lifetime.

WHEN YOU KNOW HOW TO LOVE

Love is not difficult or complicated; it is something that God formed within you as part of his perfect plan. The Bible tells us that God is love and that he first loved us. This indicates that there is already a pattern, an example established by God in how we as people should love:

"Dear friends, let us continue to love one another, for love comes from God. Anyone who loves is a child of God and knows God. But anyone who does not love does not know God, for God is love.... We love each other because he loved us first."

(1 JOHN 4:7-8, 19)

Love is an internal connection that is activated when one is attached to another person. Love takes shape and grows during the development of a friendship over time. Love turns into a deep feeling in which the heart begins to show one's feelings in many different ways. So, love is expressed, felt, seen, heard, and touched. Love is generous, understanding, and serene. True love is not aggressive or irritable. Love is not deceitful, shameful, jealous nor fearful.

The apostle John points out *that "Such love has no fear, because perfect love expels all fear. If we are afraid, it is for fear of punishment, and this shows that we have not fully experienced his perfect love"* (1 John 4:18). This means that there is such a thing as perfect love, perfect love comes from God, and it is a vital part of the foundation in a marriage.

SACRIFICIAL LOVE

Sacrificial love means giving of one's self in everything. It is a public demonstration, a total surrender, a genuine performance that sacrifices one's pride and ego. As such, within love there should be no limits or barriers to hinder the magnitude of how love is expressed. John again tells us:

"God showed how much he loved us by sending his one and only Son into the world so that we might have eternal life through him. This is real love—not that we loved God, but that he loved us and sent his Son as a sacrifice to take away our sins."

(1 JOHN 4:9-10)

This means that love is a sacrificial act that would benefit the person loved. Love is giving without expecting anything in return, just as God loved the world so much that he made the best and ultimate sacrifice for us: Jesus Christ. In essence then, true love is not just a feeling, it is also sacrificial.

"LIKE" AND "LOVE" ARE NOT THE SAME

Many may think that "to like" is the same as "to love" but that is not so. The well-known Spanish song "Loving and Liking" says it this way:

> He who loves will want to serve,
> he who loves will give his life.
> And he who likes pretends to live
> but never suffers, never suffers.

He who loves doesn't have to think,
he gives it all, he gives it all.
The one who likes tries to forget
and never cries, and never cries.

Liking can soon come to an end,
loving, however, knows no end.
It's because we all know how to like,
but few know how to love.

There is no end to love, but like is limited to time and circumstances. To love implies a total sacrifice, while to like is unwilling to give it all. To like is to pretend or conform without having to sacrifice. Love is sincere, noble, kind, tender, and eternal. In a true and deep relationship, love carries more value than like. Love never loses its value but like is something limited and lasts only temporal.

In the next chapter I will talk about the acts of love that describe the characteristics of true love. And in chapter 17, you will learn about the in-depth value of love.

CHAPTER 13

THE KILLERS OF ROMANCE

> **"Anyone living that sort of life will not inherit the Kingdom of God."**
>
> GALATIANS 5:21

Throughout my years of serving God, he has graciously blessed me with many gifts of the spirit, one in particular, the gift of discernment. The spirit of discernment has been operating fully through many facets of our ministry. In various occasions, I've been able to see beyond the natural through a person's life and have discerned deep into one's inner being. Yet, over the years, I've also seen how God has gifted my wife with the spirit of discernment, and one of the way's that she has used discernment has been to provide a way of protection over our marriage through certain individuals.

For example, on several occasions, Raquel has been able to sense when someone is not doing what is right. There have been times that she has been concerned about certain women who may have tried to approach me with less than pure intentions. In those situations, two things were very clear:

1. Most of the time she was right.
2. I generally had no inkling of the situation.

I've learned that when Raquel whispers something to me, or warns me to "be careful with that person" I had better pay close attention to her. Most women can see and sense what men can easily overlook. I'm not talking about a jealous spirit, but rather about the spirit of discernment. No person would have an affair in their marriage if they could see where that would lead to.

We must shed the disguise of deception with which sexual immorality has been presented. For King David, in 2 Samuel 11, sin was disguised by the body of a beautiful woman, Bathsheba, as he watched her bathe. At that moment, David did not consider the devastating effects of a passionate, adulterous sexual adventure: a murdered husband, a dead child, a daughter raped by her brother, and his son murdered by another brother. Adultery may seem exciting and exhilarating in the moment, but it always brings pain, grief, and sadness. Let's shed the deceptions and unmask ten Killers of Romance that target marriage.

KILLER #1: A LONG MARRIAGE IS SAFE

This statement is absolutely false. If it were true, it would be like saying that because people have lived a long life, they will remain in complete health and happiness. By accepting this premise, one can develop a false sense of security by thinking that the marriage is safe because one has been married for many years.

Statistics show that there has been an increase in the divorce rate among those who have been married for twenty-five years or more.

After all those years of raising children and pursuing careers, both husband and wife may suddenly realize that they have been going in opposite directions. They no longer have anything in common other than their children. Then, once the children marry, the parents discover that they are strangers to each other living under one roof. What they once shared in common is now gone.

The sad part about a divorce is that there is an emotional separation that takes place long before the divorce itself. Years before a divorce, emotional separation started happening between the couple that has led to the fading of love. Over the years, any apparently "safe" marriage can experience significant emotional separation.

To sustain a healthy marriage "maintenance" must be implemented. The unfortunate problem is that Christians may live with the illusion that divorce is not something they would consider to be a possibility for them. However, as they spend less and less time with each other, the spark of romance in their marriage is gradually extinguished. It is foolish to think that as long as you come home faithfully every night and have sex with your spouse from time to time, you have a good marriage. No, no, no! Think again.

Remember that physical death rarely happens without any warning. First, there are symptoms that lead to an illness, which then result in death. Similarly, the breakup of a marriage follows a certain progression. A weak marriage will turn into a sick marriage, and a sick and neglected marriage will eventually die. Don't wait until the deathbed of your marriage happens to try to do something. Watch for the warning signs throughout the journey. When someone has drowned, it is too late to call for a lifeguard. If you want a good marriage, take good care of it! Today is the day to rescue your marriage if you are experiencing signs of emotional separation.

KILLER #2: SELFISHNESS AND SELF-INTERESTS

Marriage requires for the spouse to come first. The job description for a husband is found in Ephesians 5:25 (NIV): *"Husbands, love your wives, just as Christ loved the church and gave himself up for her."* This verse can be summed up with one word: SACRIFICE. A few verses earlier, the apostle Paul presents the job description for a wife: *"Wives, submit yourselves to your own husbands as you do to the Lord."* (Ephesians 5:22 NIV). This verse can be summed up with one word: SUBMISSION, which often manifests itself in giving honor.

It is important to realize that both husband and wife in a marriage need to sacrifice and submit to each other, being careful not to make things revolve around oneself. Submission and sacrifice create an atmosphere of protection over selfishness and self-interest in the marriage. Recognize the signs of selfishness if it arises in the relationship, and deal with it in a loving manner one to the other, so restoration can happen. Nobody gets a divorce by being concerned for the needs of the other. Sin exposes a high level of egoism, so be aware of the spirit of selfishness because it can have serious consequences in a marriage.

KILLER #3: IMMATURITY

Immaturity is manifested when one of the spouses refuses to act as an adult. Paul's wise words to the Corinthians was: *"When I was a child, I spoke and thought and reasoned as a child. But when I grew up, I put away childish things"* (1 Corinthians 13:11). There comes a time in life when childish tantrums and pouting must be put to a stop, especially in marriage. Since you are no longer children, act like adults and live a full and happy life. Your spouse will love you for it.

KILLER #4: MANIPULATION

Manipulation occurs in a marriage whenever one of the spouses wants to get their own way in certain situations. A husband or wife cannot use manipulation to control or direct their spouse for personal gain. Many couples think that they can manipulate their spouse to make adjustments in their way of being. But this is not the case nor is it healthy. A person cannot use manipulation to either transform or change the other. Manipulation is a very dangerous weapon to accept in a marriage. No one has the right to control another person for personal gain. It is a sin and it should not be tolerated in what God created to be a wonderful and healthy marriage.

KILLER #5: LACK OF COMMITMENT

In a marriage relationship, it is imperative that the couple stay firm in their commitment to one another, regardless of the many issues that may arise. Each spouse must know that their level of commitment in the marriage will last a lifetime when they are sensitive in protecting their commitment. When a lack of commitment happens within the couple, the relationship suffers many consequences, causing losses rather than wins. Staying committed to their marriage means that their word matters, their honesty is valuable, their openness to each other remains at the core of their love, and commitment to the oneness of the marriage is held at a high esteem.

KILLER #6: TEMPTATION

When a husband and wife both work outside the home, with little time for each other, temptation enters very subliminally in different forms, and if one of the spouses falls into the temptation, it can kill the marriage. It is easy for a married person to entertain thoughts of spending more time with another person of the opposite sex, if the married couple is not taking the proper steps to spend quality-time together. Do not let the enemy deceive you into thinking that it's okay to open up to someone else other than your spouse. The devil deceived Adam and Eve in the Garden of Eden and they fell prey to temptation. Always find time for each other; otherwise, the possibility of temptation, and falling into it, may arise for someone else to start a relationship with your spouse.

KILLER #7: ECONOMIC PRESSURES

Disagreements regarding finances can quickly destroy a marriage. What brings a couple together, however, has nothing to do with money. When they got married, they desired to live together happily, in poverty or in wealth. Although finances play a vital role in a marriage, if not dealt with well, couples start to lose focus on a healthy relationship over financial issues. Married couples should learn, early on, to live on a budget, not spending more than their allotted income, and not borrow to buy something that is not needed. Couples should save and spend wisely. Healthy marriages agree to prioritize their spending according to their income. Wise counsel is usually needed in this area where many couples struggle to manage their finances in unity.

KILLER #8: OUTSIDE INTERFERENCE

Never allow a mother, a mother-in-law, an ex-spouse, a best friend, children or any co-workers to come between you and your spouse. Never allow ungodly people to give you advice about your marriage. Be cautious of outside interference. The Bible tells us:

❏ *"This explains why a man leaves his father and mother and is joined to his wife, and the two are united into one."* (Genesis 2:24)

❏ *"Oh, the joys of those who do not follow the advice of the wicked, or stand around with sinners, or join in with mockers."* (Psalm 1:1)

KILLER #9: LACK OF FORGIVENESS

A spirit of forgiveness must always be present and operative in a marriage. Whenever there is an argument, are you the kind of person who goes back in time and goes over past issues? If so, you are sabotaging your marriage. The past cannot be changed, so you must admit it, dismiss it, and forget it. Focus on a great future together and commit to building it with your spouse. What's more, be quick to forgive. You may say, "But what if (he or she) hasn't asked for forgiveness yet?" Jesus forgave on the cross before his murderers asked him to. Jesus said on the cross: *"Father, forgive them, for they don't know what they are doing."* (Luke 23:34). When a married couple chooses to forgive each other for wrong-doings, their love for one another always grows stronger.

KILLER #10: COMPARISONS

The constant comparison of a spouse with others is not healthy for a married couple. The risk of comparing your spouse to others is that it can lead to fantasizing about being with that other person. The following are some examples of things that are said:

- ❏ I want my wife to look as good as the neighbor.
- ❏ My husband does not meet my emotional needs like my neighbor's husband does.
- ❏ I want my husband to go to church on Sundays like other men do.

The two greatest institutions on earth are the family and the church, which is exactly why Satan is targeting them. If destroying the home is the number one priority in the mind of the enemy, who is the killer of marriages, then the home should be placed as number one on your list of priorities. Nehemiah 4:14 says: *"fight for your families, your sons and your daughters, your wives and your homes."* Your loved ones are a worthy cause for whom to fight. Fight for your family, fight for your marriage. Strong families produce strong churches and a strong nation.

Ask the Lord for strength in the aspects of your marriage mentioned in this chapter. Take spiritual authority over everything you own, and do not let any marriage killers destroy what God has given you. Your marriage matters very much to God.

CHAPTER 14

CONFLICTS IN THE BEDROOM

> **"Don't sin by letting anger control you. Think about it overnight and remain silent."**
>
> **PSALM 4:4**

Years ago, a pastor shared with me a story of a marriage counseling session that he had experienced in his office. This particular couple had been married for thirty-three years, but had not had sex for twenty years. "What happened," I asked. "According to the wife, her husband had always been a bitter man, to the point of being a constant grouch. Over time, she became so upset with his anger that she decided she did not want to have sex with her husband anymore. Her husband eventually got used to their life with no sexual intimacy. And he eventually found a lover during this season of their married life. The wife became so enraged with her husband that they even separated by sleeping in separate rooms in their home. Apparently the husband didn't love his wife, and she continued to live with him since he provided financial support for her and for the needs of the home. The couple continue to stay married to date, yet they were never happily married.

"So why did she come to see you after all this time?" I asked the pastor, "Well, it seems the husband left his lover, and soon found another lover, alcohol. Finally, she came to me seeking help because her husband had a problem with alcohol, and had been unfaithful to her in the past. She wanted to know what she should do. "What did you tell her?" I then asked him.

"I told her, "Ma'am, why do you think your husband sought a mistress and now has a problem with alcohol?" She replied: "I don't know... I think he just doesn't have any self-control."

Then I said, "No, ma'am, that's not the reason. You are the reason. If you want to fix this relationship with your husband, you are going to need to fix your attitude and forgive your husband. And then get your hair done, put on a little makeup, buy a sexy evening gown, clean the house, set the mood, and take your husband to bed. You can fix this problem."

WHAT GOD SAYS ABOUT SEX

In order for us to understand how to resolve conflicts in the bedroom, especially sexual ones, we need to review what God says about sexual intercourse and intimacy. One of the most important passages regarding the intimate relationship between a husband and wife is found in 1 Corinthians 7:1-9:

> *"Now regarding the questions, you asked in your letter. Yes, it is good to abstain from sexual relations. But because there is so much sexual immorality, each man should have his*

own wife, and each woman should have her own husband. The husband should fulfill his wife's sexual needs, and the wife should fulfill her husband's needs. ⁴ The wife gives authority over her body to her husband, and the husband gives authority over his body to his wife. Do not deprive each other of sexual relations, unless you both agree to refrain from sexual intimacy for a limited time so you can give yourselves more completely to prayer. Afterward, you should come together again so that Satan won't be able to tempt you because of your lack of self-control. I say this as a concession, not as a command. But I wish everyone were single, just as I am. Yet each person has a special gift from God, of one kind or another. So, I say to those who aren't married and to widows—it's better to stay unmarried, just as I am. But if they can't control themselves, they should go ahead and marry. It's better to marry than to burn with lust."

This passage contains two principles that are very important foundations for sexual intimacy in a marriage.

First principle: A sexual relationship is exclusive to marriage

God created the sexual relationship for man and woman within the holy bond of marriage. It is part of his perfect plan for humanity to multiply and the human race needs to participate in the sexual act because it was God's way to multiply on earth. At the same time, God established the sexual relationship as a physical act that brings pleasure and satisfaction in both men and women. Without the physical pleasure in the sexual act, surely humanity would not have multiplied.

1. The first purpose of sexual intimacy is to have children.
2. The second purpose of sexual intimacy is sexual pleasure.

Nevertheless, it seems that this situation has been reversed: Pleasure before multiplication. What do I mean by this? That there are an increasing number of people who seek the pleasure of having sex, but have no interest in having children. These individuals are basically selfish because they only think of themselves without considering God's plan. Remember that God's plan was for the multiplication of mankind before physical sexual pleasure.

The following three important points help us to see why God decided for sexual intercourse to be limited to marriage:

1. Sex unites two people as one, which is a physical reality. Two people who participate in sexual intercourse are transformed into one flesh. Joining with an unmarried partner today and another tomorrow, in sexual acts, is against God's principles. The sexual union is an act that should take place only within a marriage. Sex outside of marriage is sin.

2. The sexual relationship is intended to make the earth fruitful. The problem we face today is that people seek pleasure first, without accepting responsibility for the result. Today, young people seek sexual pleasure outside of marriage, and they call it love. That is not love, it is sin. When sex is not out of love, but only for pleasure, it becomes a problem for society when children are born out of wedlock. Children

need parents, a responsibility that is birthed with the sexual act. However, society has seen sex primarily as pleasure. Women get pregnant without being married, and their children end up living without parents as a whole. Children are eventually raised with either grandparents or other family members. Many children end up in foster-care or adoption systems and suffer the loss of their own parents raising them.

3. Sex does not begin with a physical act of sexual intimacy, but rather in the mind. The idea of having sex comes first through erotic stimulation prior to sex. Whenever there are two people who are thinking all day about having sex with their spouse, they will be ready, willing, and eager to have an unforgettable night in their bedroom. Whenever there are two people who are always angry and arguing, or those who are selfish in thinking only of themselves other than being with their spouse in the most intimate way, they may have sex every two months, but that sexual act will not be pleasant or satisfying for either of them because of their disconnection to each other and the dryness of love in their married lives.

In light of the above, it is important to nurture a relationship daily. Always think about your ways of wanting to be with your spouse and no one else. May your sexual desires only be with the person God has given you. In addition, learn to play and communicate about everything your heart desires with your spouse.

Woman, don't think that your husband can read your mind. If you feel sexually aroused, tell the man you love how you feel. If he doesn't show any interest in the moment, I guarantee that if you start touching and caressing him, it won't be long before he gets that you desire him, and he will end up in your arms, loving you the way you need to be loved.

Let's understand that sexual intercourse was designed by God to be normal, pure, and healthy with marriage. There is nothing bad, filthy or impure in what God has created. Sexual intercourse is not a sin because a sexual relationship between a man and a woman was God's idea from the beginning. The problem is that for generations, people have been contaminated with myths and lies from the devil; manipulating people into sexual immorality. This is a deception that should be rebuked in the name of Jesus; and the married couple should enjoy their sexual intimacy to the fullest.

The devil has contaminated the beauty of the sexual act, as he has also done with music and many other things. The Bible is clear that God honors marriage: *"Give honor to marriage, and remain faithful to one another in marriage. God will surely judge people who are immoral and those who commit adultery."* (Hebrews 13:4)

When it is said that the marriage bed should be kept pure or undefiled, it means that a married couple can make love as many times as they want to, where they do it and how they want to do it, it is lawful and acceptable. Actually, it doesn't have any kind of impurity attached to the act. "Undefiled" means flawless, unsoiled, immaculate, clean, and everything that a married couple does together, by agreement, is not evil.

Second principle: Your body does not belong to you

At the time the apostle Paul wrote to the Corinthians, many Greek women were being deprived of sexual relations. Their husbands were more concerned with aesthetic pleasure, and they stopped having sex with their wives. When these men became Christians, many of them changed their perceptions of beauty to their own theological way of thinking. In other words, they became so "spiritual" that that they stopped having intimate relationships with their wives. That is why Paul rebukes and tells them that they are wrong:

"The husband should fulfill his wife's sexual needs, and the wife should fulfill her husband's needs. The wife gives authority over her body to her husband, and the husband gives authority over his body to his wife. Do not deprive each other of sexual relations, unless you both agree to refrain from sexual intimacy for a limited time so you can give yourselves more completely to prayer. Afterward, you should come together again so that Satan won't be able to tempt you because of your lack of self-control."

(1 CORINTHIANS 7:3-5)

Notice that Paul writes *"The husband should fulfill his wife's sexual needs."* What then does he mean? A husband's duty is to show his wife affection. Often, when a husband demands an intimate relationship from his wife, she may feel that she is just being used for her body. Many husbands believe that wives have to fulfill their every wish. Then, once she fulfills her duty, the husband rolls over and falls asleep. That's not what fully satisfies the wife. Women need romance, they need to be kissed and held. They need to be told they are loved, they need affection, they need sweet words of appreciation and respect. Showing affection for your wife may include the following:

- ❑ Talking with her.
- ❑ Respecting her through your cleanliness when you are together in bed. She deserve a clean, attractive husband.
- ❑ Prepare the mood with something you both like, such as music, candles, lights dimmed, etc.

LEARN TO DISCUSS EXPECTATIONS AND METHODS

One of the most common conflicts that arise in the bedroom is when a couple talks about their expectations and methods of sex. In general, couples should enjoy each other in this area of their relationship. Still, remember that you both have different perceptions of how sex should be carried out. You may both have the same goals of achieving sexual fulfillment, yet have two different expectations for how to reach that.

Talk with each other. Before you have sex, ask yourselves, "What do you like? Do you like to be touched or held in a certain way?" Express your likes and dislikes. If you have no idea what you like or don't like, then it is time to explore and experience the human body. This is not the time to criticize, but rather about learning from one another.

As a husband, I need to look for what Raquel likes, and as a wife, she needs to look for what I like. We are creatures of habit, so don't get into a sexual routine; continue to experiment and explore every time you have sex, and continue to talk with each other.

Keep in mind that sex is something that is serious, but you don't always have to be serious in your sexual relationship. Enjoy yourself with your spouse, learn to play together. Don't let your married life become boring and stagnant. Learn to have lots of fun in the bedroom. The more fun you have together, the more fun you will want to have together for a lifetime. So, make it fun!

CHAPTER 15

MONEY-RELATED CONFLICTS

> "Honor the Lord with your wealth and with
> the best part of everything you produce.
> Then he will fill your barns with grain, and
> your vats will overflow with good wine."
>
> PROVERBS 3:9-10

One of the main causes of conflict in a marriage is money. It is not the sexual relationship, nor the children, nor work, nor the mother-in-law; it is the issue with finances. In fact, money is one of the most common determining factors in divorces today. God knew from the beginning that money was going to cause problems within humanity, and that is why Jesus spoke more about money in the New Testament.

Money is very essential in a marriage. The Bible is full of passages related to the management of finances and good stewardship. In fact, God wants His people to prosper and be good stewards of what he gives us. God wants us to manage our finances with honesty, he also wants us to live free of debt, and not to envy others. When a couple fails to follow God's established principles in the Scriptures, the result will always bring about strife and suffering.

Ask yourself a simple question: "What caused Samson to lose his strength?" Most people answer the following: "Because Delilah had Sampson's hair cut off." My next question then is "What motivated Delilah to have Samson's hair cut off?" Most people would have no idea – money was her motivation. The answer is found in Judges 16:18:

"Delilah realized he had finally told her the truth so she sent for the Philistine rulers. "Come back one more time," she said, "for he has finally told me his secret." So, the Philistine rulers returned with the money in their hands."

Once again, finances are very essential in life, and the Bible tells us that "money is the answer for everything." Ecclesiastes 10:19. Money helps us buy what we need to survive on a daily basis, as well as to help us enjoy life in general. In your married relationship, ask yourselves these three questions:

1. How do we think about money?
2. What do we work for?
3. How do we use the money that we receive?

Married couples must learn to set financial priorities and determine how a budget can help set future goals for the family. This will improve their quality of life. One critical question is: "To whom do our finances belong?" Well, we live in a day and age that is quite different from that of generations past. When both partners in a marriage have jobs outside the home, many couples end up dividing their income and each managing their incomes separately. This financial divide within the marriage, creates a mindset that is unbiblical.

The Bible tells us that when a man and a woman marry, they cease to be two and become *"one flesh"* (Mark 10:8). This is a phrase that is not only related to the sexual union, but also to the fact that the two have a mutual identity as a couple. Their identity is now found in a family, a home, a bank account, a budget, and an agreement with regard to how money is spent. Throughout this process, there are mutual interests and concerns that arise between the couple, and that's when they learn to work closely to reach good agreements.

Let's take a little closer look: When building a good marriage, couples must know that they both own the home they live in, the children belong to both, and cars and household items all belong to both spouses. The two of them enjoy the foods, electricity, water, and all the comforts of the home. So why does money make them drift apart?

As we have seen, the expression "one flesh" not only refers to a sexual union, but also implies "unity" since the two are transformed into a physical identity of oneness. The couple forms a family with a budget, and decide on how money will be spent. The couple shares a home, including everything in common, having the same concerns, interests, and needs. The money, then, should be seen as belonging to both. One bank account and one budget, and one in spirit as way of thinking. Paul puts it this way in his letter to the Ephesians:

"Make every effort to keep yourselves united in the Spirit, binding yourselves together with peace. For there is one body and one Spirit, just as you have been called to one glorious hope for the future. There is one Lord, one faith, one baptism, one God and Father of all, who is over all, in all, and living through all."

EPHESIANS 4:3-6 (EMPHASIS ADDED).

Therefore, if we are to make every effort to be united in one body and in one Spirit, we should make the same effort as well in the area of finances in a marriage.

TIPS FOR KEEPING FINANCES IN ORDER

Some time ago, a brother in the Lord asked me: "Pastor, how can a couple begin to earn money and then know how to begin to save?" Well, I gave him the following advice:

1. **Take control of your finances.** Place your money in a single joint account to which you both have access. Ask yourselves as a couple: "What do we think about money and what are we going to do with the money that we receive?" Communication in marriage is always important, and especially in the area of finances.

2. **Understand that the money belongs to both spouses.** Whether one spouse in the marriage or both works, the money belongs to both of them. Even if one makes more

than the other, it should all go into the couple's bank account. If managed well, there will be enough money for incoming expenses as well as outgoing expenses to pay financial debt.

3. **Analyze assets and debts.** Every couple has assets, i.e., cars, clothes, televisions, furniture, jewelry, tools, etc. Debts refer to what is owed together. The plan is always for the assets to be greater than the debts, which becomes part of a savings plan. It's important to consider what will be left for their children if God suddenly calls them home to his glory.

4. **Establish a good budget by which to live on.** Learn to spend on what is most necessary, and/or learn control spending habits if there is no budget. When a family lives on a budget, they should save at least thirty percent of their income each month; and much more if they both have jobs. In the long run, this becomes important when periods of economic crisis occur, or when there is a long-term illness, an unexpected disability or loss of employment. There should be enough savings in a couple's bank account when crisis happen to get through those hard times.

I should clarify that there is no justification based on God's Word, for a husband to be so lazy as to have his wife support him financially. Both spouses can and should work, if there is a mutual agreement. Ultimately, however, the husband has the final responsibility as the provider for his family.

5. **Married Couples should set goals together.** When I talk about goals, I refer to such things as buying a house, going on a vacation, and investing in their children's future college

years. When income is not sufficient, one goal may be to return to school in order to prepare for a profession with higher pay. Nevertheless, always make the most of your present employment, making yourself available to your supervisors for better opportunities. Take responsibility and be a witness of God's favor in your work. With this attitude, God will surely open new doors when needed.

6. **Learn how to invest and save.** Couples need to learn how to invest and increase their earnings, rather than just leaving money in a savings account that may earn only a small percentage of interest, out of fear of losing the investments in a down market. Proverbs 13:22 (NKJV) says: *"A good man leaves an inheritance to his children's children; but the wealth of the sinner is stored up for the righteous."* When a couple learns how to invest and save money, the financial return is so much richer and results in greater future endeavors.

7. **Establish a plan for spending money.** First and foremost, honor God with your tithes. Then you can save a percentage of the income while being able to spend on overall necessities. The issue with many married couples is that they do not tithe, or give any of their income to God. Neither do they save or invest. Yet, they do continue to spend on things that are not in order to a financial plan for the family. It is important to establish a plan for what is needed and what is wanted; there is a big difference between these two. The couple must agree to have good spending habits that line up with a budget.

8. **Learn how to manage finances.** Invest in attending financial seminars and buy books on money management, as there is much information available. Find Christian ministries that specialize in helping churches teach God's people on how to manage their finances and being better stewards of their money.

9. **Learn to use your credit cards wisely.** Learn how to use the money in the bank each month. Never forget to pay the bills in full at the end of each month to avoid paying interest. There are cards that offer mileage or other incentives for each dollar spent. Learn to use these wisely to earn mileage for free travel or other rewards. For example, by using the credit card and paying it off at the end of each month, one can purchase household items, pay regular monthly bills, pay tithes, and put gas in the cars. The rewards can easily come to two thousand dollars each month. Those two thousand dollars can earn twenty-four thousand miles a year toward airfare for vacations. Avoid having more than two credit cards, as too many can be dangerous in the long run.

10. **Never let money control you**. Despite overwhelming to the contrary, most people still believe that money brings happiness. Rich people crave greater riches that can be caught in an endless cycle that only ends in ruin and destruction. Couples must realize that one day, their riches will all be gone, so be content with what you have. Learn to monitor what you will do to get more money. Love God's work more than money. Love people more than money, and freely share what you have with others. Paul encourages

us to be careful with thoughts of money in 1 Timothy 6:10: *"For the love of money is a root of all sorts of evil, and some by longing for it have wandered away from the faith and pierced themselves with many griefs."* (NASB)

11. **Don't put work before family.** Family comes first. Yet there are many people who work excessive overtime hours in order to have more money, but there is always the danger of money becoming more important than family. It is better to have little in a happy family than to have a lot in an unhappy family. Guard your family and create plenty of family time together while balancing a good work ethic.

12. **Pay off all debts.** Proverbs 22:7 warns us: *"Just as the rich rule over the poor, so the borrower is servant to the lender."* If you are inundated in debt, sell what you don't need and use that money to pay off outstanding debts. That is the wise advice of Romans 13:8 (NIV): *"Let no debt remain outstanding."*

In order to keep one's finances in order, it is important to remember what the Bible teaches: *"Honor the LORD with your wealth and with the best part of everything you produce. Then he will fill your barns with grain, and your vats will overflow with good wine."* (Proverbs 3:9-10)

CHAPTER 16

AN AGREEMENT TO AGREE

> **"Can two people walk together without agreeing on the direction?"**
>
> AMOS 3:3

A t the heart of any conflict is "disagreement" or rather, the failure to reach an agreement. Reaching an agreement is the way in which a husband and wife become one flesh. That is what takes place when a couple takes their wedding vows; that is, an agreement to a set of principles that govern a marriage.

To this day, I have not seen a joyful enduring marriage without the following six basic principles for agreements in the home:

1. Build the marriage on the Word of God.
2. Leave the past behind.
3. Never stop working at building the marriage.
4. Both husband and wife need to change.
5. Agree to disagree.
6. Always give your best in everything you do.

Now, let's take a closer look at each of these six agreements.

FIRST AGREEMENT: TO BUILD THE MARRIAGE ON THE WORD OF GOD

Raquel and I entered our marriage having come from different backgrounds and abusive ways of acting in a marriage. She comes from a family of four girls and one boy. It was a family in which her very aggressive father abused his wife and children both verbally and physically. My mother-in-law was submissive to her husband, even while being mistreated. She worked very hard for her family and was responsible for paying all the bills, while my father-in-law stayed home due his physical disabled condition.

My father, on the other hand, abused alcohol for seventeen years of his life. He would come home drunk every weekend while carrying two bags of food to keep my mother from getting mad at him. While he was out getting drunk, it was my mother who took care of five children. There were even times when my father would kick us out of the house because my mother would take us to church on Sundays. Out of jealousy, my father thought my mother was having a personal relationship with the pastor.

When we got married, Raquel and I did not realize that we had brought a lot of baggage and countless hurts from the past into our own marriage. Everything about ourselves was very different from each other. We each had a system for paying bills, our food tastes were different, as well as other customs. So, it was difficult for us to come to terms of agreement in various areas because of how different our lives had been.

The example our parents had given us had not been the best for either of us. But with God's help, we were able to realize that he was the only one who could change our lives. We learned to get into God's Word to teach us his godly principles for a firm marriage foundation. In addition, we decided to set aside everything that controlled our character, our attitudes, our behavior, and anything that was contrary to the Word of God. Finally, Raquel and I agreed that we would commit ourselves to honor and respect each other in a Biblical way. From that moment on, we began to work on interpersonal changes that would create a new godly model for our marriage.

When a couple makes the Word of God their primary focus, by reading the Bible together on a daily basis, praying together, and for each other, while learning to fulfill their promises to one another, the marriage becomes stronger and resistant against any devices that the enemy will throw their way.

SECOND AGREEMENT: TO LEAVE THE PAST BEHIND

The principles of marriage are not altered based on past experience. Although there may have been hurt, mistreatment or rejection in the past, there is no special privilege to set aside any of the requirements for a healthy marriage. A wife must submit to her husband. A husband, must love his wife sacrificially, with a commitment based on his love for her. Past relationships should never dictate what one can and cannot do in a marriage.

Over and over again I see people struggling in their marriage because they compare their spouse to that "perfect" person they once knew during their courting months prior to the wedding; or they compare the way the husband treats them with the treatment of an ex-boyfriend or ex-husband. For example:

- ❏ Why don't you open the car door for me? My ex always did.
- ❏ Why don't you dress better? My ex always dressed with style.
- ❏ Why do you want to buy that car? My ex had that same one.
- ❏ My ex held me better with his arms.
- ❏ I don't like the way you cook. My ex was a better cook.

Those who live in fear because of the way they were treated in the past, as well as those who live in a constant state of comparison, will never find true happiness with their spouse. They are always living in the past or what they once had. So, they wonder, "What would it have been like if I had married the other person?" Remember that such thoughts and negative comments can only lead to an unhappy and unfulfilled marriage.

THIRD AGREEMENT: NEVER STOP WORKING ON BUILDING THE MARRIAGE

There are those who believe that if two people truly love each other, there is no need to work on the relationship. Please understand that marriage is an exceptional relationship, and in order for it to grow, develop, flourish, and be fulfilled, it must always receive the proper love, care, attention, time, and nurture.

Many couples are unwilling to work on their marriage relationship. They may work hard at maintaining the home, building their careers, keeping up their physical appearance, fulfilling ministry commitments, exercising, etc. In fact, they work on everything except the marriage itself. All these other things are important, but they are only temporary. Your spouse, on the other hand, will always be by your side, and that is where your commitment to building a strong and secure marriage therein lies.

So, what does it mean to work on building the marriage relationship? It means that the couple will learn to stay in love for the marriage lifetime. It means that you and your spouse will take the time to talk and listen to each other while learning to spend much needed time together. It means that you will make every effort to learn your spouse's passions, desires, fears, achievements, and future goals. Sometimes it means spending a little money and going out for a romantic evening together without the kids. If there is no extra money, simply going for a walk around the neighborhood or through a nearby park will help strengthen the relationship.

When you work on building a strong healthy marriage relationship, you are giving of yourself completely, and that is not always easy to do. Giving of yourself to your spouse means putting aside self-interests to simply enjoy what you have in each other!

FOURTH AGREEMENT: BOTH HUSBAND AND WIFE NEED TO CHANGE

Any growth involves change. Maturity requires change. Development and multiplication require change. Likewise, any marriage brings about change in both husband and wife. One person alone should not take full responsibility for the total change. Change must come from both.

For example, when wives come to our office for counseling, they often say that their husbands need to change. They say things such as...

- ❏ He just won't change. He's always the same.
- ❏ He doesn't show that he loves me. He's always the same.
- ❏ He won't accept his responsibilities. He's always the same.
- ❏ He doesn't take care of his appearance. He's always the same.

Later, Raquel and I would conclude from that session that the one who needs to change is the wife. Her views of change are different from that of her husband. Both spouses in a marriage are individuals from different backgrounds, so they both need to change in certain areas of their lives in order to meet each other's needs once they are married. Change involves:

1. Changing individual's stubborn wills and laying them at the feet of Jesus.
2. Accepting the counsel of God in matters of the heart concerning God's perfect plan for the marriage.
3. Renouncing all bitterness and selfishness.
4. Learning to submit all negative attitude, bad vocabulary, hot-temperament, and negative behavior, to the authority of God's Word.

FIFTH AGREEMENT: TO AGREE TO DISAGREE

Are you in a position where you always disagree with your spouse? It is very easy to fall into the category of disagreeing with your spouse because the tendency is to think first of self, and not your spouse. If there are two people with two different ideas, which is the right idea?

Perhaps the wife prefers Mexican food, but the husband can't stand it. The husband might prefer Chinese food, but she doesn't like it. Maybe you like a certain model of car, but your spouse prefers another kind. If you think about it, in a household with more than one vehicle, you may often see different models which means each has chosen their own likes.

Maybe you are a night owl, but your spouse is an early riser. The solution is really quite simple. Find some common ground for compromise and agreement between your differences. Do not expect your spouse to always be the one who has to change to become like you, adopting your interests, your lifestyle, your way of acting or your tastes. Value the differences you have and come to an agreement on things that matter on a deeper level:

❏ Eating together is more important than eating the same foods.

❏ Accomplishing much in life together, is far more important than arguing over the mundane things of life.

❏ Taking the time to communicate and discuss changes of the day far outweighs each other's independence in decision making.

So, reach the point to where you can both agree to disagree, and be willing to respect each other's unique way of thinking while maintaining true love in the relationship.

SIXTH AGREEMENT: ALWAYS GIVE YOUR BEST IN EVERYTHING YOU DO

An agreement requires surrendering one's ego. That is why a healthy marriage will always require a heart full of selfless giving of oneself. A healthy marriage is one in which an agreement can be reached every time there is a disagreement.

Many would believe that in marriage everything should be measured as half and half; that is, the husband gives fifty percent and the wife gives the other fifty percent. These people are clearly wrong. Why? Because a healthy marriage is characterized by spouses who give their all. This will, in turn, help the efficiency and help find agreement whenever there is a disagreement.

CHAPTER 17

THE FIFTEEN STEPS TO LOVE 1ST CORINTHIANS 13

> "Three things will last forever—faith, hope, and love—and the greatest of these is love."
>
> 1 CORINTHIANS 13:13

There is so much that could be said with regard to love that it would be impossible to discuss it to the fullest extent of its meaning. The Bible is very clear in providing fifteen steps to the idea of love. Most believers have read, at least once in their lives, 1 Corinthians chapter 13 which is commonly known as the *"The Excellence of Love"* chapter.

One day, as I was studying this particular book of the Bible, God showed me to focus on the fifteen steps that he designed regarding the excellence of love. In the process of studying these steps, I realized how great the power of love can be. I trust that this revelation that God gave me will be a great blessing for your life as well.

15 STEPS TO LOVE

In the United States, February 14th, Valentine's Day,[4] has been selected as a day to celebrate the symbol of love. However, the issue in our current society is that there is little in-depth understanding of the true meaning of love. Consequently, we see the steady rise in divorce rates, an ever-growing number of abortions, and increasing cases of domestic abuse as some of the major issues in our society. The family unit has been devalued due to the lack of true love. The abandonment of wives and children by husbands is something that is also becoming more and more common.

Faced with these problems, I ask myself the following question: "Why is it so difficult to love?" The answer lies in taking a good look at the following fifteen steps to love:

1. LOVE IS KIND

The first step is found in 1 Corinthians 13:4, which tells us that *"love is patient."* Before one can be patient in love, however, one must appreciate the meaning of the word love. Any standard dictionary would define love as "a profoundly tender, passionate affection or intense feeling for another person; a feeling of warm personal attachment."

The Bible, on the other hand, employs several Hebrew words to express the idea of "love" primarily with the verb *ahabah*, which has as its root *ahab* or *aheb,* that reflects a

---

4   In many Latin American countries, it is known as "The Day of Love and Friendship".

clear feeling of attraction, sexually or otherwise, and the desire towards something or someone that you want to have or be with. For example, this is how Jacob expressed his love for his wife Rachel, serving patiently for seven years to win her: *"So Jacob worked seven years to pay for Rachel. But his love for her was so strong that it seemed to him but a few days"* (Genesis 29:20). We can also see this in the expression of love for a friend, such as what Jonathan showed toward David: *"Jonathan became one in spirit with David, and he loved him as himself"* (1 Samuel 18:1, NIV).

Now let's look at the word patient which can have the meaning of "bearing provocation, annoyance, misfortune, delay, hardships, pain, etc. with fortitude and calm, without complaint, anger, or the like".[5] Paul teaches us that patience in love is paying the price for someone, it is tolerating the pressure of a problem, and resisting conflict without complaint, anger, or the like. It is very easy to say to someone "I love you" but it is not so easy to show it or live it by way of actions.

Love is more than an emotion, a feeling or an expression. To love, one must be willing to pay the price for the person that is loved. That is why love means to surrender and give of one's self to the person they have chosen to live with for a lifetime. However, love does not mean running away from problems, or abandoning an unfavorable situation or the family itself. Love is not dependent on others, nor does it play the role of victim when things do not go his or her way. It is not manipulating the other person in the relationship or sitting around and waiting for

---

[5]   The King James Version of the Bible translates the word patient as "suffereth long", which is curious since the word patient as a noun means a person who is undergoing treatment, or suffering as the result of an illness.

others to do things for them. True love fights until it wins, works until it conquers, and runs until it reaches the finish line.

If in a relationship one is not willing to be patient, it may be because he or she is not willing or able to love. The Bible makes the following clear to us: *"This is a trustworthy saying: If we die with him, we will also live with him. If we endure hardship, we will reign with him. If we deny him, he will deny us"* (2 Timothy 2:11-12). In short, patience becomes a proof of our love, and it is the reason why we never give up in a relationship.

2. LOVE IS KIND

Let us now look at the word kind which means "to have a gentle, benevolent nature or disposition; to be indulgent, considerate or helpful; to be mild, gentle." When the apostle Paul writes that love "is kind" he makes it clear that in the middle of whatever conflict, suffering, and differences may exist in a marriage, if there is true love, a person should be affable and gentle in conversation, in the relationship, in the difficulties of life. A good metaphor would be to be as sweet as honey.

Love expresses itself this way because it is what one needs during the most difficult times of life. While it may be very easy to say "I love you" when everything is going well, it can be quite difficult to say when nothing is going right. The expression of love while experiencing conflict, demonstrates pure and genuine love. Paul puts it this way:

"Get rid of all bitterness, rage, anger, harsh words, and slander, as well as all types of evil behavior. Instead, be kind to each other, tenderhearted, forgiving one another, just as God through Christ has forgiven you.... Imitate God,

therefore, in everything you do, because you are his dear children. Live a life filled with love, following the example of Christ. He loved us and offered himself as a sacrifice for us, a pleasing aroma to God."

EPHESIANS 4: 31-32; 5: 1-2 (EMPHASIS ADDED)

3. **LOVE IS NOT JEALOUS, IT DOES NOT ENVY**

The word jealous, or envious, can be defined as "a feeling of discontent or covetousness with regard to another's advantages, success, possessions, etc." It can be negative feelings toward those who possess something you do not have. On the other hand, love that is not jealous will not be looking for what does not belong to one, including frivolous and unending arguments between a couple or those in the family circle.

To be more direct, love is not attempting to steal another woman's husband, or looking to have another man's wife, or trying to shape one's marriage to be like other couples and comparing spouses with others who have something he or she wished for. Proverbs 14:30 says: *"A peaceful heart leads to a healthy body; jealousy is like cancer in the bones."*

According to Galatians 5:21, jealousy and envy is a desire of our sinful nature, meaning that when there is envy or jealousy in a relationship, it is quite possible that love does not exist. Those who ignore such sins or refuse to deal with them reveal that they have not received the gift of the Spirit that leads to a transformed life.

4. **LOVE IS NOT BOASTFUL**

The boastful and conceited person presumes that his or her love for someone is better than that of others. In our counseling sessions, Raquel and I have seen people brag about something that they are not. They attempt to demonstrate in front of others that the love in their marriage is perfect, but in reality, they are unhappy in their imperfections. Their presumption and way of thinking when confronting conflict goes something like this:

- ❏ You will never find another love like mine.
- ❏ I am the best that you have.
- ❏ No one will love you the way I love you.
- ❏ No one can give you all that I give you.
- ❏ If it weren't for me, I don't know what would become of you.

When you truly love from the depths of your heart, there is no room for boasting about something you don't have or someone you're not. When someone boasts it is because he or she has no love. The Bible says: *"Better to be an ordinary person with a servant than to be self-important but have no food"* (Proverbs 12:9).

5. LOVE IS NOT PROUD

Love is not proud, or as the King James Version says, *"is not puffed up."* Pride goes hand in hand with boasting. The person who is proud presents a high opinion of him or herself to others, generally as excessive self-esteem, but often with contempt for others who are deemed to be inferior in some way. My own definition of pride is; haughtiness and an inordinate appetite to be preferred over others. God's Word gives us clear warning about pride:

❑ *"Pride leads to disgrace, but with humility comes wisdom."* (Proverbs 11:2)

❑ *"A fool's proud talk becomes a rod that beats him, but the words of the wise keep them safe."* (Proverbs 14:3)

Love in a marriage cannot grow with this type of behavior since the person who feels superior to his or her spouse does not value the other for who they are.

6. LOVE DOES NOT BEHAVE RUDELY

In the middle of a trial, conflict or an argument, it is easy to be vulnerable and fall into the hands of the enemy. In his epistle to the Corinthians, Paul tells us that: love *"does not behave rudely,"* or as the King James Version says, *"doth not behave itself unseemly."*

The word "do" is an action verb, and it is very easy to do or say something in the heat of battle that goes against who someone really is, and not in accordance with their personality. Under the pressure of conflict, one may act improperly and begin to think about nonsense such as divorce, infidelity, verbal abuse, physical abuse, suicide, abandonment or even murder.

Where there is love, there is no room for rude behavior or speech. When one genuinely loves, one should not try to resurrect something that is already dead, something that no longer exists. Love *"always protects, always trusts, always hopes, always perseveres"* (1 Corinthians 13:7). Proverbs 3:29

tells us: *"Don't plot harm against your neighbor, for those who live nearby trust you."*

7. LOVE DOES NOT DEMAND ITS OWN WAY

When you are in love with a person, that person has their own way of acting and loving. When Paul says that love *"does not demand its own way,"* it is because there are two people with different desires and/or interests. Love does not insist on its own or its own good. Love does not think that you always have to do things its way. Love does not seek what is only good or convenient for oneself.

This type of behavior generally is accompanied by an irritating character, a provocative attitude, because everything has to be done according to one's own criteria. The Bible says: *"Don't be concerned for your own good but for the good of others"* (1 Corinthians 10:24). Genuine love looks for a way to fill a spouse's heart. There should be a constant looking for things and ways that will benefit both the husband and wife, not just one spouse. Remember that in a strong and healthy marriage, the two became "one flesh."

8. LOVE IS NOT IRRITABLE NOR EASILY ANGERED

The word irritable means "having or showing a tendency to be easily annoyed or made angry." No one is immune from being irritable around others. Any one of us can become irritated in any given circumstance. In this case, however, Paul is saying that someone becomes angry when he or she are unwilling to pay the price, to suffer, to stand the test, or to tolerate pressure. Anyone can become angry merely by wanting to be in control of a situation, but cannot because there is another individual on the other side of the matter.

Genuine love is calm, it is kind, which means that it is pleasant, gentle and sweet in conversation with another person. Psalm 4:4 says, *"Don't sin by letting anger control you. Think about it overnight and remain silent."* In other words, bite your tongue and don't say something imprudent that will prolong the argument. That is when one takes a deep breath and controls their anger, for love is not irritable nor easily angered.

9. **LOVE KEEPS NO RECORD OF BEING WRONGED**

Love is not an accounting system that keeps files of flaws and weaknesses of others. Love not only forgives, it also forgets. If God's love kept track of all our sins, what would have been the purpose for the sacrifice of Jesus Christ on the cross? Love does not hold grudges nor resentments from the past. You can't tell your spouse that you love him or her, and then when you are tested, you remind the other of what they did ten years ago. That is not love at all. If you have this attitude, you may be in a relationship merely out of convenience and for your own interest. Just about everyone has one or more grudges they are carrying as a result of having been hurt, and they may or may not know how to be rid of them. I believe that anyone who holds grudges towards others need counseling to being willing to forgive those who have caused pain in their own lives.

10. **LOVE DOES NOT REJOICE ABOUT INJUSTICE**

The word injustice expresses action this is the opposite of justice, but it can also refer to the lack of justice. On the other hand, the word justice manifests a cardinal virtue that inclines us to act and judge with the truth as our guide, and it offers to each one what rightfully belongs to him or her. Injustice, on the contrary, shows that one's actions or decisions are not based on truth and does not accord to each one what is theirs.

Injustice is not good; it is evil because it has no feelings. Injustice does not care who gets hurt or how. A friend, much less a spouse, with this type of behavior is not worth having. God's Word says, *"All unrighteousness is sin"* (1 John 5:17). Therefore, the person who delights in seeing injustice prevail is demonstrating a type of verbal and mental abuse, a character trait that is more often seen in men than in women.

11. LOVE REJOICES IN THE TRUTH

When love is sincere, it does not lie. The word truth means conformity with the fact or reality of what is said and with what is felt or thought. True love is born within the heart. It is sensitive, passionate, and sincere. Love will recognize a lie and stay away from it, keeping with the truth for the well-being of the spouse and unity in the marriage. The Bible makes the following clear: *"An honest witness tells the truth; a false witness tells lies"* (Proverbs 12:17). Truth is always timely; it applies today and in the future. And because it is connected with God's changeless character, it is also changeless.

1 Corinthians Chapter 13 defines real love. Paul teaches on the importance of rejoicing in the truth. Whenever we speak about *rejoicing,* we are thinking about a festive expression for a celebration. To paraphrase the words of the apostle, we could say "Love celebrates truth", and *truth* is born out of love. When you love someone, you will speak truthfully, because truth influences the sincerity that is necessary in the relationship. Love makes our actions and gifts useful and very meaningful in the confines of marriage and it enriches our lives for the betterment.

12. LOVE NEVER GIVES UP, IT ALWAYS PROTECTS

True love endures any suffering that is experienced in a relationship. It is willing to bear all things, to endure and tolerate what may come into our lives. In his second letter to the Corinthian believers, Paul expresses the following: *"Even when we are weighed down with troubles, it is for your comfort and salvation! For when we ourselves are comforted, we will certainly comfort you. Then you can patiently endure the same things we suffer."* (2 Corinthians 1:6)

In order to have consolation, there must first be some form of suffering that needs to be consoled. Nevertheless, suffering can also bring about transformation. It can either defeat or strengthen us, but each of us determines the end result of suffering. The trials we face result in some form of suffering, but that testing is what ultimately shapes a strong marriage. God comforts us in the process of every trial we face.

13. LOVE NEVER LOSES FAITH, IT ALWAYS TRUSTS

We have all failed to be truthful in one way or another at some time, but this should not become a lifestyle. There should never be any lies when there is true, genuine love. The apostle John gave the following words of encouragement: *"So I am writing to you not because you don't know the truth but because you know the difference between truth and lies."* (1 John 2:21)

A covenant between two people requires that there be a total trust in each other. Sincere trust is what helps to keep unity in a marriage. In a relationship there should never be the need to lie in order to cover up one's actions or behavior. In Psalm 101:7 David says: *"I will not allow deceivers to serve in my house, and liars will not stay in my presence."* Lies can only bring destruction to the unity of a marriage. Remember that the devil is the father of all lies. This type of behavior should not be tolerated within the marriage covenant.

In our counseling sessions, I have seen people very consumed by a spirit of lying. Their behavior is deceitful in nature, and the tendency to lie strengthens their selfish nature by doing whatever it takes to get what they want. King David put it this way: *"They plan to topple me from my high position. They delight in telling lies about me. They praise me to my face but curse me in their hearts"* (Psalm 62:4). Love is always trusting, but in time, all lies will come to the light.

14. LOVE IS ALWAYS HOPEFUL

The word hope is closely related to the idea of trusting that in the future things will work out for our best interests. In other words, if we have the firm hope of accomplishing something, we hope to see that the desired will come to pass. The wise King Solomon wrote, *"Hope deferred makes the heart sick, but a dream fulfilled is a tree of life."* (Proverbs 13:12)

When we love, we have the confidence that our dreams can be achieved together with the one we love. That is why when we fall in love with someone, we surrender completely to that person. We give of ourselves totally to each other because we believe there will be trust in the relationship. Without trust, it is very likely that there is no love and never will be. Nevertheless, true love knows how to wait, it is patient, not rushing to make decisions that may harm the relationship. Love is willing to take its time because it is hopeful that everything will work out.

15. LOVE ENDURES THROUGH EVERY CIRCUMSTANCE

Genuine love that is pure and true must be demonstrated through perseverance by supporting all things. This kind of love never gives up, and does not run away from a problem. Love weeps when it is necessary to weep, but also rejoices when it is time to rejoice. Love does not complain, because *"love never ends."*

Paul encourages us to be faithful to the end, even in our married lives. *"So, I am willing to endure anything if it will bring salvation and eternal glory in Christ Jesus to those God has chosen"* (2 Timothy 2:10). This truth comforted Paul as he went through suffering and pain. If you are suffering hardships in your marriage, turn to God – he promises a wonderful future in him.

Love becomes the primary basis of a good relationship as it becomes what gives us strength in the midst of conflict, trial or disagreement. Since love "suffers everything, believes everything, expects everything, supports everything," whoever is about to give up reveals that he or she does not feel true love. Always keep this in mind: *"Three things will last forever— faith, hope, and love—and the greatest of these is love."* (1 Corinthians 13:13)

As we can see, faith and hope are the fruits of love. Nevertheless, God loved us first before faith and hope existed. These are the steps to love!

WHAT IS LOVE?

> **"Love does no wrong to others, so love fulfills the requirements of God's law."**
>
> **ROMANS 13:10**

In the Old Testament various Hebrew words are translated that describe "love" or the verb "to love" especially the term *ahabah*, that has its roots the word *ahab*, which is what pleases or what one likes. For example:

- ❏ **Love toward another person,** as in the love of Jacob for Rachel in waiting seven years *"because his love for her was so strong that it seemed to him like a few days"* (Genesis 29:20). Love, then, is patient.

- ❏ **Love toward a friend,** as demonstrated by Jonathan's love for David: *"Jonathan became one in spirit with David, and he loved him as himself"* (1 Samuel 18:1). So, when we love a friend as ourselves, we give them our best.

163

❏ **God's love for his people,** as manifested throughout the Bible:

   o *"I have loved you, my people, with an everlasting love. With unfailing love I have drawn you to myself"* (Jeremiah 31:3) and;

   o *"If you listen to these regulations and faithfully obey them, the LORD your God will keep his covenant of unfailing love with you, as he promised with an oath to your ancestors. He will love you and bless you, and he will give you many children."* (Deuteronomy 7: 12-13)

We can know that God loves and GREATLY blesses those who obey him.

❏ **God's love for each one of us,** as that which flows naturally from him because by his own nature, *"God is love"* (1 John 4:8). In regard to the manner in which he demonstrates his love, it must be considered to be a sovereign act on his part.

So then, what can we conclude about love and how it is expressed?

True love is born out of our will and becomes a feeling, not the other way around. Only God loves without any effort of will, because he is LOVE in his very essence:

"Dear friends, let us continue to love one another, for love comes from God. Anyone who loves is a child of God and

knows God. But anyone who does not love does not know God, for God is love."

(1 JOHN 4:7-8)

It is through his Holy Spirit that God enables us to love by giving us his own nature:

"For we know how dearly God loves us, because he has given us the Holy Spirit to fill our hearts with his love."

(ROMANS 5:5)

Therefore, since God makes available to us the ability to love, the command that we love each other is not something difficult or impossible:

"We know we love God's children if we love God and obey his commandments. Loving God means keeping his commandments, and his commandments are not burdensome."

(1 JOHN 5:2-3)

Above all other virtues, love is what reigns supreme:

"Three things will last forever—faith, hope, and love—and the greatest of these is love."

(1 CORINTHIANS 13:13)

Love leads believers in Christ in a permanent search for the good of others. Otherwise, any manifestation of love towards God becomes unworthy.

"If someone says, "I love God," but hates a fellow believer, that person is a liar; for if we don't love people we can see, how can we love God, whom we cannot see?"

(1 JOHN 4:20)

When Christians practice love among them, they are showing the world that they are true followers of the Lord Jesus.

"Your love for one another will prove to the world that you are my disciples."

(JOHN 13:35)

Finally, let us remember that *"Love never gives up, never loses faith, is always hopeful, and endures through every circumstance"* (1 Corinthians 13:7), and that *"love covers a multitude of sins"* (1 Peter 4:8).

That is why LOVE NEVER ENDS, IT NEVER CEASES TO EXIST.

ABOUT THE AUTHOR

Pastor David Lazo has been involved in full-time ministry for over forty years. He and his wife Raquel, were founders and senior pastors of Church of Power Christian Fellowship, serving the spiritual needs of the Hispanic community in California. Pastors David and Raquel have been married for forty years, and have two grown children, Jestine and Israel. Known as "The Foursome," this family served their community church for over twenty-seven years in the City of Anaheim, California.

Pastors David and Raquel also founded Unidos En Amor Marriage Ministry over 20 years ago. They hold annual marriage conferences each year in many different countries of the world. These global marriage conferences, Amor Eterno, allow them to empower the marriage union to live more fiercely, forgive completely, and grow in God's perfect will for their lives. The hundreds of married couples that attend these dynamic conferences, receive Biblical foundational truths, and effective tools that allow them to become restored, strengthened, and inspired to live healthy in their relationships.

Pastors David and Raquel live in Colorado Springs and enjoy every moment they share with their five grandchildren; Jaden Joshua, Selah Jace, Charlotte Grace, Levi Reese, and Arielle Brave!